Neil Willis started writing at 51 years of age. Further to the success of his first book, *One Year On My Hundred*, the second, *Songs From The Mansion House Garden*, shows his development in poetry, with continuity of thought and harmonising opinion to leave the reader with more reflection. His strategy leads to a more intriguing read.

I dedicate my writings to Emma, my wife,
For her love and support.

And, to my mother, who read this book,
During her last year.

Neil Willis

SONGS FROM THE MANSION HOUSE GARDEN

AUSTIN MACAULEY PUBLISHERS™
LONDON * CAMBRIDGE * NEW YORK * SHARJAH

A CIP catalogue record for this title is available from the British
Library.

ISBN 9781398441026 (Paperback)
ISBN 9781398484672 (Hardback)
ISBN 9781398441040 (ePub e-book)

www.austinmacauley.com

First Published 2022
Austin Macauley Publishers Ltd
1 Canada Square
Canary Wharf
London
E14 5AA

CONTENTS

What is history ?

History can be different for each person.
It is loosely based around
Each country's leaders, or
Royalty, and written conflict of wars.

Songs From The Mansion House Garden

The Garden

The garden fell away from the rear terrace steps with a steady grassed-slope leading to the plateaued-lawn. Inspired by Capability Brown, the paralleled triangular beds of seasonal blooms, with knee-high hedging as edging, patterned to the far end. Studded with pyramids of cypress green, it fell cliff-like from the edge of the escarpment to the river hundreds of feet below, under wooded deciduous trees.

One could imagine Victorian children with their laced-shoes and boots, rolling longways down the embankment, arms folded into their sides, and running through the summer garden with laughter and squeals of enjoyment. From a simple game of tag to eyes hidden by hands flat, a count to ten, before seeking those that hid. The lawn of play could last all day as nannies watched over with the youngest still lying in large-wheeled, big-bonneted prams. To hide below a hedge, to run through the trees, in the age of innocence. These were the next generations to dynasties and families of royal connection. They were overlooked by the upstanding, great-grandfather Georgian mansion with arches and touches from the Italian renaissance.

The statues of goddesses, posing to the house balustrade, would stand taller than they. The children would look up to wonder who they might be, why did they stand naked with one bosom to show ? What were their names ? Young nymphs just ten years plus older, yet immortalised far beyond hundreds of years or decades.

The shorts-wearing children would pull replicated faces back at the gargoyles that penetrated walls with wide eyes and grimaces grotesque, not knowing that they were replicating some of the past history of the house, where the stone heavenly-beings that stood to the karma, witnessed the same as that the butler saw. Standing with their half-smiles, as almost a fake pretence, one could never know their thoughts, and why their sockets, no eyeballs bore.

The Wedding Dance

1.

Upon the mansion's terrace,
To the late afternoon you gazed.

Tulips sired the Georgian garden,
The June sun shone to bright.

This, one moment of our lives,
Alone you're standing as my new wife.

I'm approaching you from behind,
A waist hold, a neck kiss, … you are mine.

In the sunlight butterflies spiralled.
To the blue sky, birds sing.

Our hands swathe yellow sandstone,
The two hundred upright balustrade.

Lime trees line an avenue,
The hedges were trimmed to a maze.

Two glasses angle to a clink,
Two smiles with effervescent fizz.

Grand piano through open doors played,
To we two, a lovers' serenade.

One moment.

The crowd left for the day.

Tears to eyes that tell volumes,
We reminisce on our together-vows made.

One moment, as history was replayed.

2.

Sun down brought a moon to rise,
That sat low to easterly-skies.

We point to Venus, to Milky Way, to Mars,
Ringed-hands to the balustrade, the night is ours.

Love piano, the music to our minds,
As the wedding crowd was left behind.

Hand to hand, a half-bow, a polite request,
Will my bride say yes, this dance be mine ?

My darling wife, with hand lifting her hem,
Me, the groom, flirting jacket tail.
Synchronised feet down one score steps,
To the Georgian garden, to dance the divine.

A laced-brogue that toed,
A stiletto heel then followed ...

With your hand, your pendant, your smile resplendent,
With your lips, an offered kiss, a yes with intent.

A glint of moonlight off our wedding rings,
We, two shadows, a summer night brings ...

Your bouquet ribbon, I tied to your wrist,
A plucked rose I pin to your dress.

Oh, how treasured-hearts together sing,
Stepping to half-light, you, a temptress.

"Madam ?"
"Yes, Sir ?"
"Shall we dance ?"

A half-smile,
An eye to wink,
A titter, is a loving enchant.

"My husband."
"You, my wife."
This, from one night of romance.

'"Darling ? My hand offers a chance."

3.

We are dancing nature's piano of light,
Where the moon shines through
Fifty avenued-limes,
Where the sweet notes
Are the pulsed strings to our hearts,

We are dancing keys of black and white.

Together we promenade toe to toe,
With romancing eyes, walking slow.

Your fingers held high,
Entwined to meet mine,

Shoulder to shoulder to
The rising moon, bright.

Slowly slide to toe ...
Your beaming smile
Curves cheeks that glow.

We walk as a couple refined ...

Slowly slide to toe ...
Slowly slide,
Slow ...

We then prance on love tiptoes ...

We are dancing nature's keyboard of night,
Where your arms caress
Until we completely entwine,
Love's rhythm is dotting staff lines,

We are romancing to the heavens' lights.

We meander through the trunks upright,
Swinging our arms around
Their bark, glinting to moonlight,
The branches tip to a marriage arch,

The chorus is to our true love requite.

The stars glisten to verse fantastical,
The Milky Way ribbons the romanc-tical,
Venus glows in the evening score,
From arms stretched, to my hold you're drawn.

The look of love.
The encompass hold.
The eyes of chance.
Our marriage is born.

We are Fred and Ginger to Van Gogh night,
Lovers from the silver screen.
Stars, a celebration champagne,
With Rachmaninov fingers playing behind,

We could drink the heavens' sky bar dry.

Our shoes are playing a serenade,
That spell the melody, love made,

Each step is a note from our heart,
Each prance is a chord to our dance.

Silence will be your back when arched,
The final pose to complete enchant.

I pull you to me,
We are waist to waist,
Hands held to the side,
We glance to a glance ...

I so want your red lips to be mine.

From my embrace you unfurl ...

With quick release under my finger,
To single point you twirl and twirl.

A ballerina under nature's church,

To pirouette in the moon's glow.

In a moment I release you slow ...

Hand to hand stretched we promenade,
My hand to lapel, yours to hem raised,
Blossom is blown through the lime colonnade,
The garden scene as though marriage-made.

The mansion, stadium to our display,
Illuminates toy dancers as arms cascade,
The waiting staff whistling and singing,
Their noted presence left us both grinning.

We titter a walk of tiptoes ...

We romance under heavens so vast ...

We are stepping the piano of light,

Stepping slow,
One to toe, two and three,
Then from a rise we low ...

Come to me.

I hold you with back arched.

Enticing are our lovers' swoons.

We are vogue silhouettes to the wedding moon.

4.

Sun up, the mansion as a box for jewels,
We two, are facet diamonds,
Inbetween strings of pearls.

Georgian doors open to the terrace,
We walk out to meet the freshest morn,
Tranquility save for birds.

We stand to the warmth of the balustrade,
We stand as though king and queen,
To wave over the given Earth.

The peacocks with tails resplendent,
The limes stand as ladies-in-waiting,
The song thrush, the blackbird may sing,

But peacefulness laid over everything.

One moment.

I hold you from behind,
One loving arm over your chest,
Five fingers touch your hips.

One moment.

We remember our chance to the June moon's sight,
We shadow-danced the divine.
But now,
No more was the piano of light.

This morning overwhelmed the night.

Rachmaninov played us a serenade,
We danced as though on silver screen,
Across the garden, love was made.

One moment our shoes tapped in time.

Under the arched colonnade of lime,
The blossom confetti to the ground,
Your bouquet ribbon hung to a tree.

The wedding flower pinned to your dress ...,
As we danced the night, you were mine,
... Became a red rose between your teeth.

Remnants now lain to grass beneath.

"My husband."
"You, my wife."
To this, from one night of romance.

We have stepped the months,
Have leapt through years,
The first eyes, the kiss, to now reminisce ...

We were two shadows to the trouper moon.
Two silhouettes to Rachmaninov's tunes.

The Fountain

The fountain of opulence stood to the entrance as a turning circle for carriages from the past. The stone Adonis standing, as Mister Handsome, with a raised-arm pose above angels to their horns, and cherubs that seemed to hold the giant scrolling shell that pooled the heavenly water of truth; a shell so large that lovers could bathe in its concave base underneath bountiful waters that have been a constant cascade of joy to the years.

The god would have seen each high brow-arched to grand-spoked wheeled carriage arrive, pulled by groomed horses to a high-kneed trot, their manes tied as knots over bowed necks, their noses blowing, tired, as they got to the end of their long journies.

But Adonis would have also seen the farewells, with high-gestured waves to the departing, after ostlers had harnessed the refreshed steeds and given a steadying hand to the guest mounting to their place on the rear leatherned-seat. The hooves would play a synchronised tune to the gravel. With the open tops, and footmen to the helm, it allowed the guests one last look back up the avenue, and many-furlonged drive, to see a mansion house, that held itself so high in its esteem, its four storeys reached to the heavens. The symmetry built in stone, breathtaking. With a balustraded roof, and wording below that spelled glory to the architect in Latin giant gilded letters, if one could open the roof as a lid, one would find jewels as found in a trove or to a dressing table; the rings of kings, silvered cufflinks for earls, and diamond necklaces of gold, that lifting, splayed fingers could behold, whilst one's eyes would gaze wide in awe with mouths lowered agasp, to the boxed-riches from the past.

With its balustraded-terraces the manor sat wide to the lower floors. It perceived such a calmness that it was a building in the lotus position. There could only be peace around.

The tall décored-black iron gates with gold tips, that were the final entry, opened with their arched tops as though the wings of an angel; as an opening to the divine. With a gold-faced clock tower to match, one would need a pinch to the upper arm to realise it was all real.

From the final turn one could look back so far that the house stood in its own misty haze, as though a vision of the mind; a mirage beyond the shimmer of the heat across the view.

The Lyres

One June-time morning,
The storm rain to a sprinkling,
Blue, broke clouds to the sky.
Fresh air came to summer,
Warmth lured to our world,
The softest breeze, through avenue trees.

Sunday mid-morning,
The sun glimpsed an inkling,
We promenade, cypress by.
Shadows from limes
Angle strings as a ladder,
To play a song, of love that we please.

The garden calling,
We danced the love stringing,
As cherubs, with their lyres
Balleted the mansion.
Peering far high upon us,
You, my sunlit Madonna,
A scroll of notes matching the breeze.

Hands held, stretched,
We are rounding the fountain,
Hopping and skipping.
Blossom wind-blown through our sunlit hair.

We are skipping and hopping,
Hopping and skipping,
Our hearts singing,
Bent knees high, hands held to the air.

Manor bees buzzing,
Tortoise shells flutt'ring,
To the limes' lyre shadow,
That Mother Nature had laid.

We are skipping and hopping,
Hopping and skipping,
Hands held in the air,
Our voices singing,
Church bells ringing,
There is no stopping,
We, the heavens' loveliest pair.

Shadows sprawling,
Serenade water tinkling,
Two golden gates open, though
An angel had spread her wings.
I gave you my promise,
By the stone fountain Adonis;
Witnessing words, whispered to thee.

Towels fetched,
We are bathing the fountain,
Flirting and kissing,
Cool ankles, my hands through your hair.

Angel horns blowing,
The fresh water flowing,
Caress tunes of love,
The cascade rained, as constant played.

My lips to thy lips,
We are kissing and flirting,
Flirting and kissing,
The gargoyles' eyes, ever did stare.

We are kissing and flirting,
Flirting and kissing,
Hands flick through your hair,
Adonis winking,
The cherubs stringing,
Cypress triangles tinkling,
Angels' horns blowing,

... We, the mansion's most romantic a pair.

Kissing, flirting, lifting your skirt,
The sunlight, through water twinkling.

Rounding, hopping, skipping a flirt,
We, the highlight of the fountain fanfare.

....

The cherubs with lyres ...

Are they who inspired ...

A hand, a ring, ... a true love declared.

The Rose Garden

After luncheon, one could take a stroll through the hundred acre garden. To the side of the mansion, tall privet hedges concealed a rectangular wall, that in turn revealed the rose garden.

Some short, some tall, some to ramble a trellis, but each rose individual. They sat to their squared-beds with a formal bricked-walkway as a path through blooms that could fragrance a summer's day.

A statue of Venus stood to her podium as though a compliment to the flowers of love, that would lose their petals late-summer to leave blossom-edged earth softening the straight lines.

One could imagine the windfall heart-shaped petals might be gathered in little hands and then thrown to the air so they could again float down as though a shower of wedding confetti. Or, one could see the young Victorian lovers hold hands with slow synchronised steps. They would pause, lift a bloom between fingers and smell its sweet nose. A smile, a shared word, an adoring eye to romantic prose.

The Harpist

Behind the high hedges of privet,
Beyond the arched black iron gate
Of love hearts, with ornate curls,
Lies the secret that is a garden;
One serenaded by history's ladies in pearls.

You are my rose of the rose garden,
Serenity, after green lawns chased,
Venus plinthed to the lovers' path,
Where men could woo the prettiest girls.

Heart petals of red,
That love ever fed.

My English rose of the rose garden,
Promises are words not of haste.
Held secrets of the confined hedge,
Are ours through consented-troth,

Your words paused, my smiled-pledge.

The gate closed, nobody knows
Our hideaway, has more intention;
A titter, a hand, the eyes of glowing,
My courting, between flowering beds.

And the harp played as though it rained,
Scrolling through octaves, fingers splayed,

The harpist sits to her stool low,
Our recital, her fingers meander.
Your cheek as the wooden carved pillar,
Over the strings, her tips do curl.

We danced slow the lovers' path,
One hand to hand, one to your waist.

A plucked rose, held to your nose,
Droplets teared to petals' edge,
The stem lying thy cleaved-breasts.
A fragrance as though nature-sprayed.

Fingers feel every curve to your face,
A moment to touch what God had made.

....

As I picked Georgian roses, bunched.
As I held you close.
I saw Venus smile a while.
The bouquet, our romance, Heaven-blessed.

One moment, I received for that I prayed.

Lips hued as rose red,
Whispers heard by the love-stemmed beds.

The History

One could admire the decadence of the high society; a glimpse in awe of the privileged and titled who stayed at the mansion house.

One could believe that every relationship, every friendship, every business deal was in a sunbeam from Heaven, as the gods looked upon the so-thought righteous.

The children that played to the garden bore the innocence that every day the sun shone on their lives, without a care. They wore beautiful clothes, ate privileged foods and were tutored privately.

But, there will be considered conflicts in any household; large or small, whether single storey or three floors more.

For one to grow from nothing with very little, to achieve on one's own esteem, makes a better person; of character, of faith.

The high society set knew the title they would receive as soon as they were born. If there to be no current title or formal address, available through bequeathment, a new one could be made immediately; an instant grace was made by favour, that the lower classes or servants should look on the new child, with no qualification or reality in life, as though he be God-given and deserved acknowledgement beyond the normal person he was.

A life of hand-me-downs; from the silken christening robe, to entitlement, to money, to land, to housing. The new child would never want for anything ... except to be normal.

The Baron Heir

Curtsy to the Baron's heir,
Because the Baron tells you so.
Already subservient to he,
Spare not for his every want.

For the floorboards you clean,
Are to be polished for his tread.
Golden are his leathered-soles,
Goose down-filled his postered-bed.

Nod-bow to Baroness's son,
The Baroness signals so.
Respond to the click of fingers,
Bear to his every little whim.

Open brass-knobbed doors,
As though to the heaven, they hem.
Feathered are his ego wings,
And he returning unto them.

The child born under the golden clock,
The christening gown bore diamonds.
The figure cross to his head,
To pretence that he be haloed.

By acknowledgement of the clergy,
By recognition of the sat-king,
Marquis stands to baronship,
As the eldest son and only child.

Curtsy, bow, address and respect.
Your courtesy, never forget.

Make sure lines parallel the lawn,
A cushion to the master's carriage,
White linen to his dinner lap,
Yet he rides
A rocking horse of mane, plaited.

The floorboards that stow his tread,
Are to be his in another age,
The land to be his barondom,
And your jobs at his right hand.

The mansion house, balustraded,
To be his, on the great Baron's death.

He to inherit his grand title,
Without conscience of his pretenced-life.

He will ride his father's hunting steed,
Not knowing his elder's love-thirsty need.

Told how he shot a man dead,
The confession on Papa's last breath.

The Woodland Steps

One could hear the young children, from eras, singing simple songs and rhymes, as they descended from the garden to the river, in time. Two hundred steps through woodland trees made a counting game that used memory nous, as they had fewer fingers to hands.

The clarity of happy, in tune, under the shade of June. Trees to each side of wide divide; natural timber-edged, each an earth plateau, many feet, before a step again. Hop, skip, stop ... drop, with two flat shoes to make a stomp.

Jump, bump and giggle was the riddle.

As the children ran fast, the nannies would walk slow, behind.

In the evening, lovers, one would find, hand in hand, talked down to the waters, that mirrored in the shade to the sunset of day.

This was a tunnel of love, to the banks below, from the mansion's lawns above.

Almost stilled, so slow the water flowed. The last heat of the day, if one looked upstream, phased to a haze. The swans, curved their necks over backs, with sleepy heads. Floating on a glaze, under willow tips, it seemed that the weeping tree was resting to a pillowed-bed. Segmented-dragon flies hovered to dip and then flutter. Kingfishers glint-skimmed the water, as though taking a sip. It could all be a scene of dreams.

The squired lady might sing, whilst petals from bunched-roses, picked, she threw. "One for me, one for love, one for you." A song to the son of the sire, for whom she longed.

In the decor-gabled Edwardian boat house, was a punting boat, stored, ready to launch down the gentle slope, made for two.

The River Dream

The water reflection on a silk swathe,
The summer afternoon of love.
Elms cut shadows across our way,
The willow happy as it sways ...

We are punting the flow to the upstream,
The sunshine dapples above,
Gliding through a novel's scene,
Kingfishers glint to the haze.

Blue and orange spark through reeds.

Love is gliding,
The pole sliding
Through the glaze.

The fisher hunting,
With open beak,
Beads, his eyes.

We are punting, I stand, you to the seat,
Your roses tied to a bunch.
Squinting sun through the leaves,
White swans to the flow, sleep.

Peace is idling,
Our love is riding,
The late day sighs.

Roses you picked,
Bouquet your nose,
Your two lips hid.

Cupid flying with bow, takes his aim,
Red petals thrown to the stream,
Floating as you softly sing,
Tiny fishes through water leap.

And ballerina swans curtsy the stage,
Point wings as arms to their sides,
Flawless together they bide.
Reflecting as seven white brides.

Heaven mirrored to the tides.

Love abiding,
Ripples widening,
The banks kissed.

Buzzing wings frisk,
River breeze blown,
Long dragon flies.

Taller elms stand as men-in-waiting,

The air cut as the cherubs lyred,

The feeling that we are both free,

Willow bowing to the river's side.

Love petals become sparse divide,
Downstream passing the river bank,
Where willow touches the waters,

Kingfishers glint to the sun.

Swans float, our boat beside.

The river is the church aisle.

Fingers fan the mirrored-glaze.

A summer evening serened.

....

We are punting to the upstream,
To be figures to the sun's daze.
Where lovers fulfil their dreams.

Life Vale

The barondom mainly lay below the high-plateaued mansion house. On the vale land were cottages rented, and farms tenanted to harvest the hay.

It was almost an appropriation that the aristocracy be higher than they. The mansion house had its gardens, so formal, whilst the vale was the furrowed and normal.

One could look up from the lowland to the Baron's home as though it were half way to Heaven, where its dust sandstone glowed in the sunlight.

The tall Georgian windows were open, curtain-tied so draping to a curve, as though they formally addressed the frame, upstanding.

The balustrade hemmed the facade as though it were the pulpit edge for stage lighting. But, what could be the show, the script almost quite frightening ?

The Pantomime

We stood on Life Vale,
Stood in awe as we looked up.
The mansion house, prude, so proud
On the escarpment,
As though closer to Heaven.

The cream stone, hued,
Windows tall to attention.
The show stand of the Baron;
His stage to the world,
Drapes open to perform.

As though to God.

So, he took scene one,
Much welcomed and smiled.
The orchestra, a fanfare played.
The clash of cymbals,
The roll of the tympani drum.

Closer to Peter's Gate.

Scene two; audience
Duped by his innocent style,
He laughed loud to draw them in.
Raucous his smile.
They to be soon under his thumb.

His halo, our vision.

Scene three; the open door,
The theatre saw the blinding truth,
Sinister was his right sneer.
The lighting subdued,
Promise told, fingers crossed.

His wings now lost.

Will he draw his sword ?
His belt pistol gun ?
A dagger for the heart,
Or garrotte with tighten' cord ?

A fear, cold as frost.

To the river of Life Vale
Swim black feather swans,
The deer with timid fear,
The rabbits feed, astute their ears.

They stand to unflowered heather,
And look up to the house of treasure.

Admiring his ermine-edged cloth,
Yet considering his undered-wrath.

Inspired, he is titled clever,
The actor gained such performance laud.

....

Cottages one or two, in debt.
The farms paying handsome rent.

Money to the Baron's safe.
The king's taking his percent.

Underclasses bear such cost.

Only seen to ride Sunday hunts.
Oiled, his saddle, leathered.

....

To match his pretenced smile,
The rings he wears might sun-glint,
But, his halo lost, from The Lord.

Bow the Baron's approach,
As he rules with *many* a sword.

The Balcony

The balustrade extended to a stone round balcony that overhung the side garden many feet below. The view, to name one of a few, looked over the vale land to twenty miles forward, where trees and hedges split fields, that seemed larger to the foreground, then becoming ever more thin and wide as they met the line to the sky. The few houses seemed minuscule as though placed by a child on his make-believe toy farm set.

One could imagine a lady from past years in the hundreds, had departed the dining friends, to marvel the view as the sun set, so colouring field upon field, but also tingeing the stone where her hands might couple, or she may have sat, with her long skirt pulled tight to her angled half seat, but left freefall to a point, hemming her crossed ankles, as her one tall-heeled shoe would toe the ground. Her hair, blond, curled and long to cascade forward of one shoulder. Her hands cup the falling and stroke slowly downwards one to another, then repeating. She with a dream of love, might swoon, whilst quietly singing the simplest of tunes.

One could envisage a gentleman lover might serenade to woo her from the garden below; a stringed-tune enchanting, to their love enhancing, and she to offer a hand to join her on high. So to mouth a request, as she stood, her face sun-blessed. He, in white shirt refined, his gathered sleeves creased a line, with silvered-links the cuffs held. Smiling, half rye and a glint to his eye, why would he refuse his princess's friendly behest?

To the witness of Greek nymph statues that adorned the terrace, under the still-posed cherubs that played lyres upon the mansion house, and to the reddest of suns that blushed their faces, he could have whispered his love sincere, as his left cheek flirted hers, his chiselled lips tickled words, to the listening bejewelled-ear.

The Jewel Box

To the sun, as it set on the trees,
Strauss's waltz was just me and thee ...

We are whirling the balustrade of time,
Two Viennese lovers turning clockwise.
Three steps to turn to the counter,
Your dress hem held, up to my side.

The sun downing, to dark, your face fades,
We, dressed to the grandest ballroom charade,
Joining hands, my request replied,
Split from the mansion great masquerade.

Each baluster is to a year gone by,
Attentioned, as soldiers on the parade,
To Strauss smiling, cherubs lyred,
We, cyclone wind to the time line.

We are dancers twirling
Of the jewel box opened,
With waltz music tinkling,
As the glint of earrings.

The delight of a child's face,
Merry, as we go around.
Velvet red, dress inlay,
Servants to the master's tray.

We are furling the red sunset skyline,
A Georgian couple to the terrace glide,
One hand held high, one to your back,
We fast-turn as though a tea cup ride.

The V birds, backings,
To make-up puff clouds,
The mansion a mirror,
As the last song thrush sings.

The terrace, open drawer,
With stone trinket gods,
Roman pendant urns;
Pickings for fingers, as we turn.

The sun as a whole ruby,
Stars, night diamonds,
A balustrade long chain,
Necklaces, gold, beam the sky,

Eye shadow colours draw the lines,
Make-up pencils cover the wide.

We two dancers curling
The mansion doll's house,
It, hinge open-fronted,
As a box to the kings.

We are
Waltzing dressing tables
Of ladies to earls,
Face oval mirrors
To clasp up dropped-pearls.
To dynasty wives
With rings on fives,
To the fair maidens,
Their earrings, laden.
And
Witness to waiting-ladies
Of history queens,
Who stringed corsets
Behind zed-folded screens.
To champagne sipped
By high-rouged lips,
Lovers of princes,
Their carat necklines,
And
Grandees, so graced,
Cleavages, delicate-laced.

Ladies wearing Asian chintzes.
These, the historical lauded times.

We see
Waiters in doorways,
Spinning trays up high,
Filled cocktail glasses,
Point toes, synchronised.
Butler platters, silver,
Morceaux in slivers,
Serving plates, laced,
Finger foods of taste.
And
Drawn tall drapes, pulled by
Chamber pinafore-maids,
Who plump white pillows,
Folding bed sheets, laid.
Nannies to babies
Sing soft lullabies,
Doormen polite-nod
As grandees retire.
And
Chefs plumed in white,
End buffet service, clean down sides,

Gents, dress shirts, black-bowed,
Velvet jackets, smoke long clay pipes.

The dynasties, princes, kings, queens,
In the air of the mansion's serene.
We dance to the meetings,
The dignified greetings,
The affluents, linened-tables, beseated.

Pens of signatories,
Words of dignitaries,
The grand presidentials,
Greater influentials,

The guest-listed essentials.

To the prime ministers,
Authors and great actors,
So humbled benefactors,
Without bare credentials.

We are dancers hurling
Through the history of time,
Whirling, to twirl and swirling,
To the balcony curling.
History of the enriched,
Of the entitled,
Privilege classes,
The wealthy masters;
Barons,
Lords,
Ladies,
Earls,
And the public-empowered:
Envoys,
Ambassadors,
Chancellors,
High ministers,
All with their hands, so well endowed.

We are waltzing Viennese,
Turning to the counter ...

Stockinged red dress muses,
Being show piece charms,
Giving no excuses,
Cupping their client's arms.

We are waltzing history,
Spinning time again,
We are coasting
To the money-go-round;

The curtsies, the bows,
Ceremony toasts,
The hand shake-greetings,
Kiss-cheeking one's host.

Meeting new heads of crowns.

The right ayes, the just-sos,
The 'don't you knows',
Knowledge bequeathings,
Back scratching meetings,

Evening to night, more so loud.

We are waltzing to mysteries,
Up-pointed noses,
High-fingered poses,
Much quaffing whilst scoffing,

And their many 'oh so prouds'.

The business offings,
Non-clever boffins,
Those newly sir-knighted,
For donations, requited.

The each one invited,
The over-exciters,
Those of such talents,
Whom play their recitals.
History of high-browed,
Beclothed-poseurs,
For the great snobs,
Who shoulder-rub nobs.
Classies,
Prudes,
Dandies,
Dudes,
Dressed in their excesses.
Luvvies,
Teasers
Flirtatious
Crowd-pleasers,
Conning cheer smiles, of their successes.

They are donning their masks,
So we never do ask.

The masquerade of eyes,
A charade of replies,

Politeness of such family ties.
Yet,

Children from lovers,
Affairs behind doors,
Forsaking all others.

But never was love the single cause.
The women, used as easy whores.

The masquerade of denial,
Charades of mis-trials,

All to contain their upstanding-pride.

We are unfurling the mysteries,
Unravelling histories.

Unknotting traditions,
As clever magicians,
Though fanfares be played,
As applause to our trade.
History of moral unhealthy,
Inane desires,
Those, less divine,
Of laundering crimes.
Slave drivers,
Treacherers,
Racially inert,
Crime perverts,
All to fatten their gluttony purse.
The unlordly,
Unpriestlies,
The sinners,
Gloating at dinners.
Their oh so formal graces rehearsed.

We're dancing to the counter,
To call and renounce them,
Waltzing ... to the classes divide.

Behind the mansion facade,
They act
Gregarious,
Vivacious,
Luscious,
Flirtatious,

As though they're unaccountable
To the whole of the nation.

....

There are creases in the sheets,
On the beds of the elite.

With glamour insincerities,
False pretences, inherited.

With make-up of vulgarity,
Such clarity to non-charity.

Your families entitled,
As though heirship be vital.

....

There are many weeds to your Georgian garden.
Splendid roses, to be no royal pardon.

....

Your characters, rambunctious,
Your life thoughts, presumptuous.

The drapes are dark curtains,
That block views of uncertains.

Ladies don lips of chewed wasp,
Gents dare not think their virility lost.

You have no box for confessions,
They be the mind-church for lessors.

....

Your history's lauded, even applauded,
Yet one's left with a different impression.

One's snooty renditions,
With such emphatic precision.

....

We are reading between lines,
Of centuried-book spines.

History of tenacious titles,
Carriages, well-bridled.
Elite ascension,
Of covert convention;
Right Reverend,
Right Honourable,
Your Majesty,
Your Highness,
As though some heralded-divineness.
High society,
High governance,
Grand mansions,
Grand ballrooms,
Heirs, graces, no place for one's shyness.

....

Curtsy at the end of your dance.
Bow to the lady of your desire.

Fingers underlay fingers,
As such politeness lingers.

Your status shown by your rings,
The diamonds to thy necks lie.

The gowned-serenade is not just for tonight.
Pomposity is a mask.
The charade played ... throughout your lives.

The Downstream

A scream broke out on
The sand hole home bank.

A shrill heard so loud,
Elms stood startled.

The small child had ran
With a face of surprise,
The sun in his eyes
To catch the kingfisher's spark;
The electric blue glint,
As he darted to fly.

The turquoise volted
Low to the river's swell,
And, before one could tell,
He taken by the fastest stream,
His body as flotsam,
Down the storm's tides.

His plight ignored,
As nannies talked.

From his home of Heaven,
The willow, arms low,
Tried to hold the flow.
The boy dragged to harm's Hell,
His distress to downstream,
One heard quieter cries.

Salmon swam up course,
Their frightened minds, torn.

The Baron's child was never found.

His epitaph; a statue to the balustrade,
It bore the same eyes ... as when he died.

The Serfs

As they polish the grand stairs' rails' oak,
There is the quietest talk.

As they sweep, for the Baron's heir, floorboards,
They each make knowing-eyes.

As they dust, the great crystal chandelier,
Down their noses they do peer.

You can see them sneer.

For the young girl, darker curls,
Wearing less of a cloth,
With her hand-down shoes,
Will never get to inherit,
Without her own merits.

For she'll have no party frock,
Though she runs beside,
And she'll seek and hide,
To her nanny she's tied.
Whom her mother is, unclear.

Brought to the mansion house's porch,
Late the day she was born.
In Baron's horse carriage,
She bore outside of his marriage.
The arrival, a surprise.

No blue to her eyes.

For the pinafore chamber maid,
Who, the beds had laid;
She, young, of firmer breast,
Suddenly left under duress,
Seen leaving in tears.

Or so it appears.

As they lay silver knives to the table,
The last place is undressed.

If they have to be quite polite,
Only her pinafore was white !
As she opened his drapes,
The Baron, already awake.
As she served him morning tea,
Apparently, he felt the need.
With groping hands to her bust,
He laid the damn wreath of mistrust.
For she was the Saturday treat,
Her image form in his sheets.

As they clear the grand table after service,
They ignore the girl's needs.

They upbring the bastard child,
Though the Baroness is riled.

Ignoring his little indiscretion,
Still upstanding, her elite impression.

They still stare with mouths agape,
Surely, it couldn't have been rape?
As she cleared away his tray,
At the pantry, she didn't say.
To her knees, cleaned his floor
Maybe, she's his paid-for whore?

As cloths are rounded to brass doorknobs,
They peer through gaps to hinges.

The prettiest of the children,
It can't be she's just God-given?

His wife drinks with strewn lips,
The Baron, shy to the stage's slips.

The Hunt

The white gloves that adorned hands,
Thrown as a gauntlet to the maiden's man.

....

Hunters of the hunting lodge,
They ride to find fox or deer,
With black boots to knees,
With tails to their jackets,
They gallop fields, over hedges' span.

Hunters of the lodge's hunt,
Gather as the sun rises,
Mounted upon thy steeds,
With hands to leather reins,
One could hear the frisk of horses.

Lodge's hunters to the hunt,
Baying-hounds of the pack,
Scamp under gate, through trees;
Low to ground, on their haunches,
They bark to the scent of fox's clan.

....

A certain lady rides dawn light,
Side-saddle to the lead huntsman.
The only one following the bark,
The only one plaited-hair to back.

And the Baron's wife kept in the dark,
Taking breakfast back at the mansion.
Not to know husband's hunting spirit,
He follows scent of foxy maiden.

For the triumphant bugle's note
Is not the strict sound of convention.
As he disrobed her tweed, knitted scarf,
And offered to remove all her tack.

....

Hunting lodge's male hunters,
Know the Baron's tradition.
He, lead man of the reins,
As sun rises to the vale,
He's lead player on riding away.

....

Late morning, back to the stables,
A brace of pheasant for the table.

Husband to the side-saddle peasant
Knew of the Baron's whispered-tale.

....

Lodge's males of morning hunt,
Knew her husband's fuelled-
Anger for the secret engage.
Hooded, as the Baron gained
A little more than blank faces say.

....

Silver cutlery laid for luncheon,
Crystal glasses to toast their success,
Children were cleared from the garden,
So
Two rivals could meet for a duel.

Back to back, centre balustrade,
The sun beat down at just gone midday.

To be seen would not be so pleasant,
Neither's anger could be at bay.

....

For the Baron acted the stallion,
The filly led on by her bridle.
The Baron, full pelham, couldn't abate,
Thought the maiden may be in season.

For he, with fancy dressage steps,
To the filly's shoulders, sidled,
She was brunette with her plaited-mane,
He, well-groomed for one good reason.

....

Men with rifles, not on parade,
Walked ten paces to either way.

They turned when two shots were bore,
Butlers and statues, as witness, saw.

The Baron's success, more than a brace,
His lover, no Puritan, of straight face.

....

Wolf hounds bark to stable doors,
The heat steaming from open breaths,
Claws scratch down the damage wood,
They clamber to air of newer stench.
Sweating is their messed chest hair,
The chamber echoes loud, incensed,
Their tails bound off the walls,
Snouts smell fresh blood beyond the straw.

Black birds fly the rookery's nest,
Straight lines angle to the skies
With a noise of them scared, intense.
Two shots broke Sunday silence,
Screams from what the butler saw,
Beaks dart forward not to look back.
To fly against flight of hundreds,
Would be the devil's double dare.

Horses bang hard-hooves to floors,
They circle fast within close squares.
Agitated, tossing their heads;
Eyes wide as though beyond sane.
Noses drip as nostrils flare,
Manes ruffled random, immense,
Half-rearing as though they are tall,
Discontent wind blows the boards.

....

For jealousy can have the greatest wrath.
Fury, from the accounted mind well spent.

The riding gloves that held the reins,
White to the balustrade, ... shot gun-stained.

....

So, true love can be fight for survival,
The rival tempted by the beauty's scent.

The Slow Carriage

Black, the carriage, when every man cried,
With glass view windows, six long, four feet wide.

The hooves to the driveway, slow,
Footmen, no emotion shown.

Arched-wheels as astonished eyes.
The noble mansion physically sighed.

Slow crunch of gravel be the sound,
He walking well-trodden ground.

Baron, betrothed to his wife's ringed-hand,
Yet, again saddled the wife of a man.

For with the adornment of such wealth,
Less becomes the discretionary stealth.
To live with support of so many riches,
He has such rights to ever endeavour,
To morning hunt and catch his Sunday prey,
Is adding to his mind's boxed-treasure.

....

For he was the man of many loves.

He played peacock, splendid feathers,

.... Then played foul to the vale's heather.

....

Adonis, god of the fountain,
Held his pretentious smile.

He, witness to the funeral cortège go,
The fountain crying such tears to the pool.
On the coffin's lid with gold handles,
Were one laundered pair of white gloves ...

The clock tower struck twelve low,
Golden face without a glow.

As though nothing had ever happened.

No duel, no gun shot, no drawing of blood ...

Placed atop the deceased, box-measured,

With enactment ... they be two sleeping doves.

....

His memory, the victim fell with a thud,
All was for the housemaster's pleasure.

The Willow

Why does the willow's head hang so low ?

To the water does he pray ?
As though he needing repentance from the priest ?

His head so, not since Sunday,
But since last month, last season, every year.

Does he know all that's flowed,
That tells his story, own guilt, a held fear ?

He has no friend, no love celebration.
Loneliness, the hardest life known.

His long hair, cast to flowing,
His head hidden, cries the incessant tears.

To life past he is weeping,
The waters, flooded, as pain increased.

Why does his head hang so low ?

The elms stand tall to side,
Heads to the sky, they as though without a care.

....

Pass by him, sparse red petals
Floated, downstream on the mirrored-flow.

Were they to the river thrown,
By a widow to her husband deceased ?

Her emotions be cast
To nature's great waters, released ?

The heart plays strong commemoration,
With death, if all love was not sown.

Was the bouquet disowned,
By a lover, an apology spurned ?

Anger thrashed the stems,
The damned-petals thwart to The Thames.

A face, grieved in moonlight,
The watered-mirror, to the upset known.

The tears, the lines, the crevice eyes.

The mouth, as hands wretch-ed hair, plied ...

....

As clouds rolled a scorn of grey,
Were bluebirds to the ruddied-skies flown ?

....

The prop of tragedy cast the last scene,
While the fat lady, her operetta cried.

To the darkened floorboards slumped,
The veil, the black dress, crumped.

The curtain fall, respects the deceased.

The last dagger to the tapestry, sewn.

....

The cob stood to his haunches,
Wings to high, as though feathers grown.
Stretched neck, bill to low,
And blew fast to frosty air.

Is love true forever ?
Or a baying crowd of bloody lies ?

Thunder Rose

You, the thunder rose,
Twisted to life's trellis.

Sitting to the north's shadow,
Little sunlight to you thrown,
And you wonder why you've not grown ?

You are passing the diamonds,
That reach to the higher sky,
That form a perfect pattern;
They stand tall, equal wide.

The persistent rose all alone,
Life's thorns to your side,
Sprawling, do you know the way to go ?

With buds as though lips, pursed,
Sad veins through leaves as sewn,
Tears roll to pointed tips.

As life's weather collides ...

Drip, drip, drip.

....

Lightning strikes fast as though,
The forlorn actress, to stage strobes.
Haunted, her face cold-grey,
Fright shown, as it be cursed.
The devil close in wings to side,
Nose hidden by arm of cloak.

To draw red as you grieve,
Sucking all he can relish.

....

The trellis rose is losing grip ...

Angle jewels happy with their home,

There's no fragrance to your thundered-woes.

Fountain of Joy

In the peace of the mansion,
To the Sunday moon,
I awoke to soft owl hoot.

With a coat over clothes,
Crept out the front door,
With a slip of my shoes.

Down the driveway of gravel,
Crunch-footsteps that travelled,

Water reflects stars,
Adonis, under a full hue.

Oh fountain of joy,
Fountain of joy,
Celebratory, the water falls.
Oh fountain of joy,
Fountain of joy,
With a hope of a penny,
How love doest me call.

Every drop be love I feel,
To pooled water, her face revealed.

Oh fountain of joy,
Fountain of joy,
Love be a mountain, ployed.

Through the avenue, her voice to me,
Through the roses, feel close to me.
As the sun sets, it's her face I see.
A dance to the lyres,
The terrace we waltzed,
Hand held to hand,
Made her my choice.

I could offer her the cottage life,
Where beds of roses bless the garden,
Fruit trees, heart-shape apples.

Oh fountain of joy,
Fountain of joy,
Love be never destroyed.

She's seen the plateau of kings,
How could my ring be best her desire ?

My hand gathers pebbles,
From the pooling of truth,
Though the water's ripples
Distort the picked proof.

Moon shimmy as water breaks,
My hand magnified,
As the stones, it collects.
But thirteen, not unlucky,
Each gemstone glistens,
Each plays its part,
To the fountain's steps,
I make my pebble heart.

Celebratory the water falls.
Oh fountain of joy,
My heart, to the moon glows.

The Last Dance

The last dance is back through the angel gates,
You to accept my offered-hand that waits ...

Toes to the gemstone drive,
Hearts to the mansion's time.

Dancing to the glories
Of history's stories.
To gilded thrones,
Which we condone.
The plateau of kings,
The garden of queens,
Peacocks are jewelled,
White swans' bills, rouged.
Blossomed, the trees,
Sapphired, the skies,
Fountain of crystals,
Gold cherubs, smile.
The plated-clock face,
The epitome of grace.
Angel gates' wings,
To Heaven, hinged.

The past relived
With garnet heart-eyes.

....

As we wear our wedding bands,
We remember our vows;
Never to squander,
To never wander,
Be there for each other.

To each, one true ring,
Says one true thing.

Your pendant to heart,
To never depart.

Together, two feet,
That can dance a rhyme.

To waltz three beats,
'I love you' in time.

....

The high ceilings,
High brow windows,
High society,
Give no greater pleasure,
If born as their norm.

It is easier to look up and want more,
Than look down at the possible less.

....

We are dancing,
With a single mind,
Our heartbeats aligned,

To be grateful for how we are blessed.

The Life Drive

We drove away from our weeks' stay at the mansion house, following the avenue to pass around Adonis one last time. Taking the same path as carriages from the past, we looked back through the angel wing gates, at our little bit of Heaven, where the hands on the gold clock stood in time, to realise the past's virtual sugar-rimmed cocktail glass had at times been spiked by the devil, high-rouge lips were not always glossed, and black bow ties lay crumpled to the bottom drawer. Also, life's river has both an upstream and downsteam, and the fountain's waters are so loud that we only see the stage's facade rather than hear the ghosts of its cast. The long drapes are tied agape; half-open, half-closed, so we cannot quite see everything behind.

History is a theatre stage; with a full orchestra together with its instrumental solos, its uplifting crescendos to the inevitable tragedy. Yet, we stand with eyes of awe, wanting to be part of before.

But, we did dance the divine.

One moment.

Me, your husband.

You my wife.

We punted to the upstream, passing trees that stood tall and proud, and those that wept as they bowed ... two silhouettes to the future's haze ... rose petals buoying in the wake ... to where lovers hold their dreams.

... Others will see history
As their family descendants;
The immediate 3 generations
And then tag the great
Grandparents for good measure.

Each generation will teach
The youngers of the
Dangers of life, but must
Also point out the good;
To always have something
Optimistic to look back upon.

Roundabouts and Piers

The Double Take

The memory of the waltz of horses,
The steam organ; a one man band,
Circling to the Christmas fair,
Parents beside, stood in pairs.

I was travelling to speed of light,
My mouth open, became a smile,
Holding tight with an inner fear,
Could one hand release without tears ?

The roundabout man had an ever-smile,
The parents were laughing as I rode by,
Other children shrilled upon the ride,
Why me, the only one, fear inside ?

I'm only going one way,
But not knowing where I'm going.
I can hear the band play,
I can see bright light displays,

But where are my parents ?

Eyes keep looking forward,
Then to the outside.
Hands clutch the reins tight,
Onwards he strides.

The thrill of the roundabout,
Onwards he strides.

Eyes keep looking forward,
Then to the outside.
I moment to see Mum and Dad,
Their hands waving high.

They are calling my name.

I just keep looking forward,
Then to the outside.
I'm only going one way,
I can hear the band play,

Dad is calling my name.

My horse comes around again,
I brave them a wave.
I've beaten my fears,
I look to the rear.

I'm ... waving hello,
I'm waving goodbye,
Mouthing the words;
Saying hello,
Saying goodbye,
Waving hello,
Waving goodbye ...

A perpetual smile of the carousel ride.

Every child was doing the same.

....

Each adult thought comes around,
Memories we've saved,
They go back through years,
So hold them so dear ...

Life is a roundabout ride;

Beautiful gold horses,
With twisted poles aligned.

Welcome the born babe,
To lose loved ones so near ...

Whisper hello,
Whisper goodbye,
Relive each hello,
Regret each goodbye ...

We're striding forward,
Only going one way,
Not to know where we're going.

Beautiful gold horses ...

Each memory ... a tear to our eyes.

Hold the love of your parents ... as though they're still here.

Regret ... each goodbye ...

They're still calling your name.

Look up to the high ... you should be doing the same.

Sunrise to Sunset

1.
I remember,
The merchant's striped canopy,
The sea's waves to my ears,
The promenade in front of me.

I'm recalling,
My parents buying ice creams,
Grandparents sitting to a wall,
Hot sunshine beating down on us.

The family laughter.
The family's love.

There I was a small child,
The world seen through innocent eyes.

Tongue to cold vanilla,
Teeth through the cone's crunch.

My grandparents walked the sand,
My Mum and Dad then following them,
Me, small beside, holding their hand.

Always looking forward,
Sometimes looking up.

I looked to tides.
Looking back, was the merchant's sign.

Elders would ever understand,
Dear grandfather looking back at us,
Mum and Dad to me, their little man.

Everything to mind;
Was looking back …
The red and white canopy,
Vivid to my eyes,
And
Beyond families walking in lines,
The ice cream merchant's optimistic sign.

2.

As I became a young man, teen age,
My tempers challenged the gauge, ...

I'm thinking,
My grandparents walked ahead,
My parents followed unto them,
I stood steadfast, folded arms.

I'm suggesting,
Ice creams were thrown to the grains,
Buckets and spades to the blue.
The child was turning to a man.

I, the young man, standing far behind,
My thoughts ignored, to my rage.

I had no care for family ties,
Not needing to hold hands to guide.

Teenagers ever understand,
Parents' ideas of the sterile kind.
Grandparents live in ancient times.

Sifting my mind, I didn't look back.
Wanting to break the crash of the tide,
Needing to prove my life was confined.

Thinking my thoughts are better planned,
To progress faster to the water's line.

I was wanting to run beach sands,
That lay front of the promenade,
Away from families pacing in tribes.
My youth no longer inside of me,
My hands could insult society.

My fists lashing through the family cage.

The merchant's was just a dull sign.

....

Generations walking lines,
Grandparents with curve hands,
Parents, shades to their eyes,
Kids, beach balls, held beside.

Generations walking lines.
Nose to tail, as donkeys on sand.

Generations walking as tribes.
Losing their senses of real time.

3.
As I became a twenty-plus man,
I could make my own better plans.

The beach was mine, girlfriend to side,
Cocky, queueing the merchant's line.

The largest ice cream, holding hands,
Not noticing the other clans.

The sands were lovers' dreams,
The sun hazy, as though make-believe.

I had become more optimistic,
Than the merchant's fun ices' sign.

Loved up, kissing.
Ice creams dripping,
Hand to hand slipping.
Cold blue sea dipping.

My hair was greased,
My thoughts released,
Love, would never cease.

The whole world was mine.

4.
Then a parent to a small boy,
That I held as my pride,
Crouching, smiling, pointing at ...
The striped sun shade canopy,
The merchant's sign fixed high.

For I shared the taste of vanilla,
Helped him make the loudest crunch,
Wiped his chin as he ever-smiled.
He was young me, just in that while.

And as we walked, slow, the promenade,
My parents, necks arched, in front,
Looking back at me following,
I held his hand and looked down ...

And I knew I would see ...
He momentarily looked up,
Then to the sea's tides,
To turn head, looking behind,
A stare at the ice cream man's blind,

Highlighting the optimistic sign.

His family genetics ran through our tribe.

5.
Now a granddad sat to the wall,
My walking stick leant aside,
My eyes are failing,
I read finger to braille,
My health is ailing.

But I'm smiling as I hear the waves,
I hear kiddies play to the beach,

Their parents correcting them;
Families, ... walking as tribes.

But even though it is beyond
Where my sight can reach,

I smell the warm wafers.
I can taste cold vanilla.
The sound of the crunch.

And though I no longer have teeth,
I'm imagining ...

The ice cream merchant's big jolly smile,
Canopy, striped, scallop-edge hems,
Buckets hung with inflatable toys, ...

Fisherman nets, floating sea buoys,
Young lovers kissing as sunset nighs,
My family, now grown, on their own.

Grandparents would ever understand,
The theory of our promenade plans.

And his chalk-written optimistic sign.

The Six Senses Pier

Our life from child to end
Is a world of our five senses.

The Christmas fairground held more than could tell,
Carols played through Tudor house streets.
The roasting chestnuts served in bags,
Were second to the temptation smells.
Together we gathered in crowds,
The noises through the many hundreds.
Lights against musical gold horses,
Merry, we all went around.

From the toffee apples we licked,
To the largest sugar candy floss clouds,

The light through pink cumulus glowed.

The seaside promenade held one more spell,
Victorian long pole, twisted, striped rock,
Wrapped in clear plastic, untwist the ends.
Balloons gathered on strings to sell,
Multi-coloured as though sunlit, proud.
Families played in their thousands,
Bathing suits, standing in the tides.

From the sand castles we'd build and kick,
To the longest shorelines that we would run.

Haze sunshine through parasols, thrown.

...

And now I stand on the manhood pier end, there
Is nothing but emptiness looking forward.
The sea bays as it laps below gaps,
Tentatively I walk the boards, sick.

Through one pebble of thought to sea tossed,
As one tear balls ... to my cheek glossed,

I've come to realise, beyond
All I've felt, ... all I've seen, ... and my ears heard,
The good and bad have been tasted and smelled,

Death's cost, ... means my whole being is sapped.

Beyond the icing on life's sweet cake,
Where blown wish-candles were just as fake,
After pink cumulus floss has been picked,
Toffee apples ... and ice lollies licked,
I was left with a real huge sense of loss;
Life reality ... being grey clouds and sticks.

I shouted "love you" against the sea wind.
It blew back coast-bound, back passed my ears ...
Nobody to hear it.
Nobody to feel it.

It blew back to the promenade of lights,
That glowed across the long canopies, striped,
Where children enjoyed cone popcorn minutes,
Striped rock hours and fairground days,
Mine drowned ... by the crash of the waves.

Nobody with real time,
Nobody to heal time.

"Love you," back to sweeter-tasting years.

The End of The Ride

One spring morning I suddenly awoke,
I drove to the seaside, to the quiet of the prom.

To the chilled blue skies,
Cumulus, hemmed the sea's line.

The waves softly lapped
To the sleeping beach long.

As the sun rose to the dawn,
My childhood was reborn.

Rising coloured skies
Transed cotton candy cloud ...

The same pink from my childhood fair.

I saw the crowds, the roundabouts,
My parents were standing ... just there.

My right hand raised to wave.
A pause.
My fingers slow to bend,
While the words were mouthed ...

"Hello."
"Goodbye."

The runway to my childhood,
Were the boards to the pier end.

Light pranced my heart, my mind,
My soul, ... my being, ... my very all.

I whispered "hello"
With tears to my eyes.

And in the crackle of the pebbles,
As the sea receded through

I smelt warmed chestnuts,
From the pop and spit wood.

"Love you," I called.

I knew you heard it.
I knew you felt it,

As sunbeams strobed the sky.

They were fairground lights,
As I saw the steam organ glow.

I heard both your voices,

The sympathy, empathy,
The soft of love console,

The elations, for birthday
Wishes to be a whole.

....

We are only going one way,
And ... I now know ... where I'm going.

I want to mount the most gold steed,
That can canter high above high.
With one hand to loosen' reins,
One constant wave saying hello.

My Pegasus as a carousel horse,
Gold twisted poles line my course,

After my body has died.

I'm waving hello ...

The end of the life-about ride.

And the next morn,
A new babe will be born.

I'll look to the rear.
I'd have beaten my fears.

To the world … I'll whisper goodbye.

….

There's no return ticket for one more time.
So, as the steam flute band plays,
I will relive, … all my years,

… By riding, the forever-sky.

In a world of complex history
Made by a complex mankind,
Every person is vulnerable …

Mother Tree

Piano Keys

And as piano keys played through his mind …
His depression stood aside.

Just for a moment.

Calmness led him through autumn woods,
And places came back from his childhood.

Just for a moment.

And piano keys played through his mind …

All anxieties were pressed against the wall,
Mind yoga took to the floor.

Then the lights dimmed.

Spotlight on one man curled in a ball,
Who thought that he was no one at all.

He's in woodland …

Streaming-tears down cheeks blurred his view,
Mind hell in the copse's glade.

Then frighten set in.

From beauty of his surrounding world,
Into the dungeons of history he is hurled.

He's past bedtime …

Accumulation of thoughts built the brick wall,
Head-hell would never it climb.

He's screaming from hurt.

Remember close times and young as child,
From a fondness of love, to hate he is riled.

It seems like hours …

The horrid thoughts circle the gerbil's wheel,
Nightmares that can never clear.

He's running for life.

Fevered-thoughts cyclone wind from hell,
A moment's sleep before the morning's bell.

...

Piano keys that played through his mind,
To hammered fists, as thoughts still remind.

Mother Tree

In morning light he returned to The Bois,
And saw yesterday's man down in the dell.
Great love and extraordinary desire,
Was a failed mission, as his life was on fire.

On orange leaves walked sorrowful-slow,
Looked to the sky through neighbour crowns,

.... A sapling, ... he was beside his Mother Tree,
With no words ... but love ... she respected he.

One step forward he hugged Mother Tree,
Face sided, with cheek pressed to her bark.
He cried and cried, fell to kneel and hurt,
Blood-grazed skin, and wiped tears through dirt.

From a man of form, to mind so wild,
From an adult's head, to eyes of a child.
Enactment fell to his begging knees,
Eyes of white seemed tortured to bleed.

....

The whole of the woodland heard one man scream,
A noise, so sharp, as it broke autumn dreams.
Exasperation rebounded the trees,
From anger, to whimpering lips of pleas.

....

On fours he had his head in her leaves,
Splayed fingers, tear-wet foliage on floor.
Hand to hand, grabbed fistfuls, tight-clenched,
Blood red eyes, as life's heart was wrenched.

Never had man such excruciating pain,
The loss of his mind to compel him insane.
Leaves under his side, curled in a tight ball,
From family man, to the sapling did fall.

Calm now ...
Calm now ...
Calm now.

He came round from a sobbing wreck of a child,
Rose with grey cheeks stuck with fallen leaves.
Dark lines under eyes, as valleys could fall,
Mother Tree saw man ... who was no one at all.

....

And the whole woodland heard one man's scream,
That rode through breeze, to break the serene.

....

Autumn leaves fell as to comfort his cries,
Wood pigeons thrashed towards the sky,
Roe deer bounded away from their clearing,
Foxes stared, statues, to what they were hearing.

Just in that moment.

Mother Tree 2

His fingers touched spring leaves.
Through light green, she splayed her veins.
In slow motion pulled away,
Felt love that was unexplained.

With curved hand felt her girth of trunk,
Her outer husk told him all she was.
Slowly, lips kissed her bark,
Much needed, love, was his cause.

....

Holding a branch of his Mother Tree,
He rose at four to greet the morn.
Both listened to the bird choir,
Their beautiful moment, ten past dawn.

Then he walked away to the top of the dell.

Right arm rose, slow spiral-hand turned,
In air, he felt the shape of the tree.
Hesitated, ... clenched his fist,
Then pulled her love, into he.

Purse-kissed his closed fist of love,
Pulled away, from his lips to yearn.
Hesitated, ... threw open splay fingers,
Such love to her he returned.

....

And the foxes were still sleeping,
The roe deer lied with eyes peeping,
The curled rabbits nuzzled in burrows,
To his lonely room ... he'd see her tomorrow.

Just in that moment.

....

In his dreams he saw forests of trees,
That saw mankind as minions of need,
That thought Mother Earth as theirs,
Taught by preachers of Gods in the air.

Mother Tree 3

"Good morning Mother Tree on such a nice day."
He really did feel good, as he walked down the dell.
When he finally saw Mater, ...
His mind darkened, ... and light heart suddenly fell.

The man raised his fists with enragement,
Eyes screamed, without thought, tears of pain.
Child-like cried for Mother Tree,
Anxiety released to his mater again.

He pummelled his Mother Tree fist by fist,
Shouted loud rage, both eyes bulging to scream,
Recited what was in his head,
Such venomous words, to utter extreme ...

Such acrimony to his mind deemed,
Much sacrifice of his health seemed.

....

And the whole world heard one man bereave,
That rustled the leaves on the empathy trees.

....

Calm now ...
Calm now ...
Calm now ...

He curled around the roots of Mother Tree,
A foetal position, the comfort of child.
One hand raised to touch her side,

He cried and cried, ... until all tears had dried.

Mother Tree saw one poor man insane,
Allowed him time to recompose again.

....

Woodland breeze blew leaves as a sheet,
For comfort, as foxes lay at his feet.
The song thrush flew away on his wing,
Morning mass heard a single bell ring.

A single bell ring ...

Ring.

Ring.

The choir lead stuttered to sing.

Just in that moment.

....

In his mares he saw woodlands felled,
That saw humans as wantons of greed.
No thought to the land laid as bare,
Capitalists that flaunted nature's fares.

Land raped to build concrete blocks,
To show their ever-consuming powers.
Religious edifices as ivory towers,
Ghastly gold doming over their prayers.

Mother Tree 4

Year goes to year, as time had gone on,
He visited Mother Tree at The Bois.
With the scent of bluebells in May,
The cool shade when summer was hot.
At the top of the dell, looking down,
From earthen smell of autumn leaves,
To the silence of the December air,
With snow laid, he stood in coat sleeves.

Just for that moment.

Mother has not aged, together they grew,
Upright she stood through the seasons.
Grey hairs that all his decades show,
Are the grown-scars, that life had given.

....

As the sun fluoresced through leaves,
The song of the freckled thrush lowed.
To recognise the times that they met,
On her trunk, silken ribbon, he bowed.

It's their little moment.

As the sun red-coloured the trees,
The sapling child looked up to high.
With one hand, on to her mighty trunk,
With love tears, ... he kissed her goodbye.

....

From Mater's comfort he would now be free,
Although he'd remain part of her family tree.

The deer looked to him from fruit bramble,

The foxes with white cravats, wore red suits,

From a single song thrush, came a chorus,

As though the woodland ... gave last salute.

Just in that moment. x

....

And piano keys played through his mind,
As his depression was left aside.
He walked away, to bear new grown fruit.
From a single tune ...

His mind concerto ... became absolute.

....

In his eyes he saw the world actually breathed,
That came to know nature's resolute truth,
Where wind as clean air blew,
Knowledge spread through plagues of seeds.

Every nation only took what was needed,
And gave back even more to nature's cause,
A scene of pink blossom,
As though mankind made forever vows.

... Vulnerable to the debates, the wars,
The rules of millennia,
Of which most are about money,
Possession of wealth,
Or the doctrines of religions.

The Wood Kingdom

The Birth

In the dawn light of March,
A feeble cry broke all peace.

Bore of the loins,
Born for love.

He, greeted by the sun,
Through the canopied-leaves.

Born to the world,
Born to the equinox,
He, the season's prince.

His feeble cry hiccupped.

Bore in his father's upped hands,
Cradled in his fingers.
Lifted toward sky, high.

Born to glade of blossoming-trees.
A thank you to his Mother Earth,
Hear the heir-to-be cry.

Hear the new heir cry.

Scent of woodland green.

Where silence lingers.

No one would believe ...

Over hedgerows.
Beyond forests of green,
Panning the fields.

Over the deserts
Where sands lie swerved,
And no life can yield.

The coastline sea,
Spanned across oceans,
Where the tails of whales
Navigate the fjords.

Through bluest skies,
Wings of wide curves,
Great albatross fly.

To steppes of grass,
Winds blow across vast,
No trees to cut one's sight.

Each person should know,
Why the heir prince ... of the March spring ... cries.

....

And so he shall be called Equinox.
The day of birth, his character.
For equal day to night,

Equal dark to light.
The perfect balance.
The child of pure mind.

His family, society-bereaved.

They live to woodland,
Kingdom of leaves,
To greener fields.

Beyond villages,
Passed all the towns,
Bells of cities.

Beyond peoples,
Beyond families,
Through communities.

Considered thoughts,
Protests of others,
From peacetime quiet,
The years of great wars.

Anarchy of sides,
To blank others' views,
Where walls divide.

Battles of death,
Where nobody can win,
Yet heroes of both reside.

Each human should know,
Whether black or white,
Religious or non,
Why the heir prince ... of the equinox ... cries.

He born not just to a world of hiccups,
Where imams,
Where priests,
Where leaders,
Focus the minds.

He born to a world of constant detest.

Where most forsake their real freedoms;
Their freedoms from ties.
Freedoms so they can personally decide.

....

For his home is the woodland of kings,
Where crowns minaret the new prince of spring,
The legend roots to hundreds of years,
The founding of life 'side the hundred of meres.

Faith stands in hard wood of pillars,
A grand temple of love that nature brings;
Young saplings as candles to the altar,
The berries as food of life to its peers.

....

The ancient woodland of the north,
Stood to witness the wasteland, south.

Field-long, just two acres wide.
Minarets and domes, west,
Towers and tall spires, east,
Yet the land was no-man's divide.

In the shade to clouds of gloom,
Land that stood furrowed brow,
Yet the sun shone to either side;
Above each religion, sky of blue.

Each, their own true peace.

The wood family washed
From the mighty hills' stream,
That passed through forest, ancient.
The same praised by the Islamics,
As being the most-holiest tide.

At the river's delta, due south,
Christians fished the reef,
Islam, their nets, released,
Along side, though a promise to cease.

The river of life met the sea's mouth.

....

His altar is below the branch arches
To sing thanks for each equinox to pass.
The autumn fruits are his larder's forage,
Abundance for long cold winter's storage.

He stood on the edge of his wooded-home,
To stand higher upon the knowledged-tome,
To view across baron land that'd been raped;
Towards the people's cities of religions,
That pray for peace of the million minions.
The spires, the towers, minarets and domes,
Yet, they look at each other with such detest,
To look upward that their god be the best.

....

There are fractures in great Jerusalem's walls,
Common foundations over religions, sprawl,
The same blocks are scribed to one and all,
Then rewritten for each reverend leader to call.

Can the spires, towers and synagogue halls,
Hold hands together to show love for all ?
Can gold minarets, stepped-temples and domes,
Kneel the same pile and respect each one's thrones.

For there are fractures in Jerusalem's walls.

The Podium of Life

The king of his own Wood Kingdom,
Nurtured the equinox son.

The prince to have life of balance.
A boy to man, must grow to stand.

To the woodland floor lay a felled tree;
A straight beech one hundred feet long.
To one end its roots still to the earth,
Now stands as a podium log.

"This my son is our altar of calm,
 The stage of two hundred years,
 With more knowledge than you'll know,
 Each ring holds teachings sewn.

 Upon its heart, feelings will grow.

 About us son, our temple of light,
 A glade to the great tree, felled,
 With midday sun coming due south,
 There's karma to the woodland's mouth."

 ....

And young saplings as a parade of candles,
A fire stood, centred-point, as a teepee,
To the north of the glade stood straight the elder;
She, the highest, was the great Mother Tree.

 ....

Equinox stood bare foot to the altar,
Two feet higher, a prouder being.

Mother Tree, she stood silently behind,
His shadow cast to her large rooted-ground.

"So, my son, here you will balance
 Your own mind, your own heart."

The prince stood straight
With arms wide, as though a cross.
But this was no religious symbol,
Or punishment for doing wrong.

"So, my son,
  Turn your palms up, hands cupped."

The prince did so.

"Close your eyes; the view of the dark."

"You are now the scales of character.
  In your left cup are sadness, anger,
  And every bad thing you now have.
  In your right palm is gladness, wellness,
  With all the good your life does bring.

  When you have more bad things to the left,
  Your mind must put equal happiness right.

  And when you have equal good to the bad hand,
  It'll be easier to stand, arms wide.

  If you have more sadness and badness held,
  Your arms will drop with the heavy hurt mind."

  ....

"Now son, touch all fingers above head,
  Allow your elbows each side as bent.

  Five fingers to the five others bend,
  Should have whiter tips that press to flat.

  Push them, eyes closed, slowly upwards
  So flat palms meet, then splay fingers.

  Your hands will slowly part at angles,
  The gap between widening as they grow.

  You have made the symbol of the tulip,
  Its spring bulb closed, opens to warmth.

Your hands will be rolling to your wrists,
You represent the springtime's sign."

....

"So son, sit to the podium,
  Your two closed feet also to your seat.

  Both your knees tight to your chest,
  Embrace your arms around your legs.

  On your knees rest your forehead.

  Close your eyes.

  You are an acorn so small,
  A nut that is not yet born.

  Slow to your feet rise,
  To stand to your podium high.

  Your hands also rise slow above your head,
  To splay wide; dangling to each side.

  And with your eyes still closed,
  You now represent ... the mighty oak."

....

The father laid a plank to the tree, felled,
Two metres wide, one forward, one to the back.

The prince sat one end, his father the other;
A pivot, the blank to tree's bark.

"This my son, is the seesaw of respect.
  Whatever you do, I, the opposite.

  When you are low down, I am higher up,
  When you are up, I'm to my toes.

  And you smile and laugh when you're high to sky,
  And have a sadden' face, when left to ground.

Every move you make, sudden and fast,
Affects my position as complete contrast.

This my son, is the same in your life.
Never be quick in responding,
To leave the others despondent."

The father then changed the length of plank,
Now four metres wide, two fore, two aft.

They balanced the seesaw, longer by length,
High to low, to the middle, then back so.

As the prince pushed his feet to the ground,
His father glided from higher to lower.

So much gentler than the prince would expect,
Less weight, moved his father, though shorter legs.

"So, my son, use the wider plank in your mind,
When you consider others in your eyes.

Wider means slower action, time to reflect.
A better balance of heart, of mind, of soul.

This my son, is one balance of life.
If you do feel higher than others,
Never laugh, they might be suffering.

Balance the seesaw as respect,
So you both sit to the middle;
Then neither is the higher,
So, neither is the lower,
And each of you have the same view."

The Balance Tree

The equinox heir played to the trees,
His homeland was the edge boundary,
Sprawled with defence bramble,
To under light, grew the weeds.

Never to go to the wasteland running between
Domes to the west, spires to east,
From ancient woodlands to north,
The heir found intrigue as fatal greed.

For he prayed on the wind-felled beeches,
As though a tight rope, stood one leg straight,
One leg balanced out to the side,
His hands cupped, high as they reach.

This, his karma to balance his mind to free.
His body a self-temple to the sky,
To keep outside, the world, wronged;
Karma beyond the religious preach.

....

Just after the morning's rising sun,
The religious war, again, begun.

He heard imams call to prayer,
As though a voice in pain,
Not understanding what they said,

But as each preached to reach,
From the east, came Christian bells.

Both heard across no-man's
As though a strength of contempt.

As the sun of low rose,
The spires pointed shadows as detest
Over no-man's breadth.

As the sun set low, west,
Minarets and domes shadowed homes,
Casting no-man's as theirs.

In between, guns from either side,
Shot across divide, banned to highest sun.
But even though the brightest noon,
The land held a cloud of gloom.

Each day, each week,
Each month, each year,
Daily, the holy fighting resumed.

But as he balanced to his tree,
He heard nothing.
Thought nothing.
Saw nothing,
His whole soul as free.

From a nurtured acorn,
He, the mighty oak, could just be.

Equinox, the self-church,
Had created his own mind temple,

Just in that moment,
There was no world beyond he.

....

Each day, each week,
Each month, each year,
Religions' solid foundation stones
Were vulnerable prone.

As though a tremor quake
Shook the earth's ground,
There were fractures in religions' towns.

The Lessons

Lesson 1

You should live your life
As though a spring meadow of flowers.
Thrive in blossoms the proud stems hold,
Scythe the long grasses in heat of summer,
Listen to the sky lark's happy song,
Gather from hedgerows, autumn fruits,
A winter woodland, buried nuts to roots.

Lesson 2

You should play your life
As though standing on a pavilion,
Your characters are one playing team.
See them all as your own mind's home pitch;
A winning run shouldn't always be goal,
But one to throw ball, one for the batting,
One to take defence, one for the catching.

Your own conscience should be the umpire.
A known win should not always be prized.

Lesson 3

You should feed your life
In small portions, a little a time,
For greed is never a need or wanting.
Life's best are fruits hanging to trees,
Afternoons for nettle tea and rest,
Enjoy sweet finger from the tree that hums,
Never gather the circle when fungi comes.

Eat moderate, allow nature to thrive.
Cut all the branches, your food tree will die.

Lesson 4

You should feel all love
As a bird sings to the blossom tree.
Collect as a bee to the nectar flower;
Make honey so you have more to give back.
Hold all love in your mind's straw basket,
Scatter it as seeds to your life sewn,
Water with compliments and watch it grow.

Your own beating heart will then rightly know,
Don't always catch, as it's better to throw.

Lesson 5

You should think through life
That a word or a gesture to others
Can be a page of the Thesaurus.
There are so many ways to convey.
Never shout at or threaten another.
Talk as though you would want them to receive,
Defence is not a good way to believe.

Your own tongue will learn to what you achieve,
Their own eyes should like what they do see.

Lesson 6

You should wear through life
No fixed hat, trouser, other dress.
To offend one of religious order,
Or mimic their everyday beliefs,
Is considered Wood Kingdom offence.
Allow them prayer, their choirs, their spires.
Allow them domes, minarets higher.

Religion makes its own enemy.
Let us not be the one under their fire.

.....

My son, our load will not have the perfect road,
There are great flints along our path,
But it is the only way, ... that we will know.

My heir,
There are cracks through which you can fall,
But,
There are large cracks in society's halls,
And
Greater cracks in Jerusalem's walls.

Jerusalem's Walls

The minarets were shadows to the morning sun,
A glint of gold as the rising shone,
A glimpse of hope for the new day dawning ...

Yet,
The imam's call to prayer,
Sounded as a voice in pain,

A call heard over no-man's,
Over the Christian east.

Each mosque, their own loud haling,
Each with individual wailing.

The domes dark vast curves as the prized light begun,
Their image silhouetted the sky;
A shadow to peoples as an awning.

The holy river still flowing,
Changed to red in sun's taint.

The callings hailed the pain.

Prayer mats lay to the east,
Looking to the towers of priests,
Who's churches looked away,
As their own congregation prayed.

The bells as an ornate calling.

Then the silence.

Any person could stand in no-man's
And dance the furrowed lines,
To chance to the southern side.

Each religion at peace,
A few moments
Where the fighting ceased.

They were all doing the same.

Dance to the sound of peace.

There are great cracks in Jerusalem's walls,
Where the foundation stones are the knowledge for all,
Where spires meet the minarets and domes,
Yet, each church is on its constant own.
Each is a threat to one another.

Share your incense and hand others your beads,
Let them feel worries of your looped seeds.
Only then will each religion so understand,
Each high fortress no longer be manned.
Each human to become a brother.

Share ever blue skies of never-ending peace,
Where every head bows to a common priest.
Every footstep to follow each in the sand,
The fisher nets are cross-fanned,
To water, thrown for one and other.

No-man's is every man's need,
Where golden wheat is the common feed.

Each to eat the harvested-bread,
Each to share fish from blue seas.

Pray under the gloried-dome,
Read from each leathered-tome.

There are great cracks in Jerusalem's walls,
Where there is room along the Western's tall.
Ask why the Jewish men, Torah to their hands,
Cry, as from their holy place banned.
Now for centuries they have suffered.

Give to them your worry beads,
One and all to touch their wall.

How does it feel ?

Does the empathy flow
In the morning's sun's glow ?

Arms to each man's shoulders,
Together smile, dance and chant.

But you can't !

....

As dew laid to the leaves ...

A promise could be a relief,

But each leader, each teacher,
Each church's lead preacher

Proclaim their disciples' thoughts;
Each with its own slant.

....

There are cracks,
Fractures, that break the mould.

Damnations,
History facts to be told.

There are great cracks in Jerusalem's walls,
From the apostles of the Dead Sea scrolls,
Translations to suit each and one's own;
Each church to have its finite brand.
One whisper begins another ...

Starts a rumour towards trouble.

Swinging is the boat of incense,
Is it there to cover the stench ?

You may as well break your beads.
Your worries are beyond their need.

Peace may always be the prayer,
But the context hides an under-layer.

Launch your ever caliphate,
As martyrdom becomes fate.
Then count the troops
Who died in your holy war ...

Your congregation ... less than before.

The imam's voice sounds of pain.
And will do each sun-rising day.

You all pray towards the east,
Yet when the sun sets to the west,
Then a thought ...
Have you done your best ?

Let the walls of Jerusalem fall
To a level praying field for all.

The imam's voice hails the pain,
Yet the land of religions ... is still maimed.

....

In the quietness of morning prayer,
Equinox fell to their lair ...

For he ran south through no-man's,

With the need to want to think higher,
He ran with toy plane in his hand,
Arm up high,
Propeller-driven by rubber band.

With engine noise through his mouth,
Over banned land launched to the air.

He thought,
During prayer, neither side cared.

....

As the chalice was passed.

As prayers were said upon mats.

As holy incense was waved.

The giving of ceremony bread ...

In the want for peace,
One landmine was released.

The furrows in their lines,
Became a crater grave for Equinox' life.

The Torah became torrid,
For something so horrid.

The Bible slammed as liable.

And
The Quran's eye for an eye,
Saw religion's ugliest smile.

....

The king of Kingdom Wood,
Put a cross by no-man's plain,
Where his son and heir was slain.

The cross was not a religious belief,
But the scales of character,
That naturally leant far left,
As it held more badder than bad.

To his knees, his father wept.
Looked to the skies,
The minarets and spires.

To know, just like his family before,
He, there, bereft because ... of the holy war.

....

The birds as an arrow head,
Flew, silhouettes, to the west,
V - shaped, as the bloody-sun set.

But it was not V for victory,
Just a b-line from man's destruct cause.

The Sloughed Cross

To no-man's stood commemoration,
Handmade from beech, almost as defiance.

As there was all bad to none of good,
Lurched to left were the character arms.

The Aquarius rain blew through the trees,
Taurus clouds charged across the fields.
Bulls, heads down, thundered the earth,
Pitted by hooves as forward they barged.

The wooden cross stood as a defiant tee,
Arms outward to lightning cross-shafts,
To contact the lords of the season's mirth,
To pray to furrows, was lottery's chance.

The rains speared an angle torrid.

The hungered-acres now a flooded slough,
From yester's sods to a famine found,
So little would ne'er feed diets of sparrows,
Layeth dearth, loss to agrarian gods.

The mud, an invite for a wallowing sow,
On brighter day she would so proud slumber.
Now pelted by vengeance of storm arrows,
The hell of weather, to pink flesh 'd prod.

As though the ground slain, and then left to bleed,
The blood flowed as a sacrificial sea.

A vow of war from Mars to never cease.
Utter umbrage as the devil laughed.

Through detest storms, one felt the pain.

....

Pointed minarets to the west, glowed.
The spires as high, flashed in the east,
The arches of gold, a smirking gloat.

Yet through the hours of the rain horrid,
One witnessed no tolerance to cease.

The poor child, a sacrificial goat,
With the longest knife ... over slitted throat.

....

So, no-man's population increased.
Shame he's there as war-deceased.

The start of life can be simple.
Look around you.
Your child will learn to replicate it.
Some colours are natural.
Others, with just a mention,
Mean so much more than
'Just a colour'.

Colours Of Life

Colours of Life

As a child
It started as a blank sheet of paper.
To the table, a small pack of pencils.

You told me that everything that I drew
Would be the many colours of my life.

Green was the front garden drawn
With a brown tapering-path.

The house, also brown, with four windows,
A chimney and a centred-door.

Then a bright yellow sun in sky of blue,

I thought for just a moment

And coloured a huge rainbow, paper-wide.
You told me it was the archway to Heaven,

With every loved one I had known,
And so every one who had died,
Had passed through the rainbow,
And were smiling the other side.

Each day I
Looked at my drawn colours of life,
Now brass-pinned to my bedroom wall, high,

And questioned, in my head, what you said ...

Why did the rainbow's mouth look so sad,
How could they be happy, when they were dead ?

I grew through my life, going school to school,
The drawing packed in an attic box, kept,

And each rainbow that I saw, though a few,
I remembered your words,
And my colours I drew.

Monday's child's kite, a diamond, red,
Tuesday's child an orange frisbee flew,
Wednesday's ran sand, golden yellow,
Thursday's hands swathed grasses of green,
Friday's boy dived waters of blue,
Saturday's wore a shawl, indigo died,
Sunday's children played under violet sky.

....

There in my mind, a prism of colours,
Arching so high, the day that you died,

And I saw you pass through to Heaven,
Looking back, you were waving, fingers wide.

At that moment, I remembered, the
Colours of life poem, you had taught ...

Red is for garden roses,
Orange, the melting sun, set,
Yellow, meadows of buttercups,
Green, the breeze through the trees.
Blue, the seas where dolphins cry,
Indigo, feathers to a bird breast.
Violet, the petals, bookmark-pressed.

I stood beside a lake of stilled-blue,
The reflection of the rainbow, a smile,

That made me think of you, happier, blessed.

My childhood painting taken from its box,
I drew the lake to the house's front lawn,

And passing through ripples of its blue,
A mimicked high arch, of my colours of life;

The colours of the world I knew ...

Garden Roses.
Melting sun, set.
Buttercups.
Breeze of trees.
Dolphins cry.
Feathered breast.
and
Violet petals ... to my conscience, pressed.

Reflections

I'm chasing the bubble
On its journey to the wind,

Running to grab the elusive bubble;
A mirror sphere of my troubles.

....

The face in the bubble was me.

I glimpsed a view as it blew,
In the breeze, it teased.
Blown through a wand, to wander,
A rainbow corona hue.

Summer clouds, the skyline threw,

Yet,
They swirled, as a storm curled,
An oil painting, turmoiled;
A perfect cauldroned-brew,
My image in the bubble's world.

My being, to the sky hurled.

The bluest blue of summer, high,
Yet, I'm in the storm, torn.
My portrait getting smaller,
To meander, free-form, to the sky.

As I looked left and to the right,
Each bubble, huddled,
I saw my face replicated,
Many, many, tens of times.

A flotilla of large and small.
Each one a reflected double.

I'm chasing the universe of troubles.

My life as a world of storms.

As other children ran and smiled,
As they jumped and laughed,

My sad portrait in renaissance oil,
Of a great biblical scene.
As Heaven cherubs lyred,

My heart just cried and died.

....

The world of troubles that I feel,
Are the burdens made very real.

....

And yet, anyone looking at me,
Would see rainbowed-freedom in dream-filled eyes.

Flying Kite Hill

I've seen the rainbow on Flying Kite Hill.
Are the highest diamonds flirting the air ?
The arch colours to the landscape, still,
Yet their streaming tails don't compare.

Is the gluttony that we yearn
A temporary tease, there to please,
As something so high, we wonder why ?

We stand at the roots of the hill.
Can we walk straight line, easy to find,
Or the winding path, the route marred ?

Many a dreamer has tried.

We can find Flying Kite Hill,
But the higher we climb,
We are still grabbing air,

The rainbow always above us,
Far beyond our tiptoed-pose;

Something far beyond the hilltop in sight,
Or the jewelled-diamonds' flirtatious flight.

A fantasy at which we stare.

The dark clouds are slow to go,
The chasing sun shy to show.

It will eventually rise to Flying Kite Hill,
Its appearance part of the thrill,

But,

As we anticipate the wait,
Where impatience is never late ...

Why are we looking for gold
At the end of the rainbow ...
When there are obvious jewels already there ?

The kite flyers are holding their dreams,
That fly temperous winds of life;
Some holding shorter strings,
Some, longer leads, to Heaven, high.

But when the time is trite,
And when such reality bites,
They see their grounding flights.

The higher they fly,
The faster they dive.

The wanton diamonds torn in despair.

So,
I gathered everything I could see,
Just because it was considered free.

The daisies plentiful
As a rash to the plain,
Dandelions as a yellow bold,
The shine of buttercups thousandfold.

But then I climbed the promise hill,
Wanting to find something more rare;

Something that would only be mine,
My selfish nature wanting more gold.

Then I realised ...

The hill was actually a mountain,
There was no straight pathed-line.

The few trees that bore my need,
Became a dark forest, I couldn't see.

I felt the hunting wolves prowl,
And in beauty of the full jewel moon,
I felt their breaths as they howled.

The mountain then became a cliff,
Something so steep I couldn't climb.

I looked up to the rainbow's tempt,
Looked down to the ravine below,
The thundering water dangerously flowed.

But far beyond all that I could need,
Became jealous of kite flyers' dreams.

I got to the peak of the promise hill,
The rainbow still higher above,
The kites flew to it, as though in love.

I asked the flyers the way to the gold,
Were they happy with just diamonds they hold ?

...

They just looked at me and stared.
They didn't understand what I could see.

They didn't realise they held diamonds.
They didn't look for the rainbow's hoard.

They felt freedom of the freshest air.

The flyers were on the promise hill,
Because it determined their wanten will.

The kites judged the wind of the day,
The rainbow told of showers on the way.

Their dreams were not for great jewels high,
But for the weather to be both wet and dry.

For they had ploughed their acres of plain,
That were vast view across the vale,
And if the wind blew the coast leeward rain,

Their own prayers would be simply real ...

Acres of ears of wheat would sway,
Stippled across the harvest month fields.
Rippling before the scythes did raze.

This was their yearning for gold,
With rainbows crossing the yield's sky.

....

I'm standing alone on the kite flyers' weather hill.
And
Even though the rainbow occasionally shines,
Tempting pots to the end of its arch,
I now imagine fields of wondered gold,
Ever precious, each ... and every day.

The kite flyers fly above fields for grain,
Where their blessing is the breaking sun's rays.

The Northern Lights

As mid-December was nigh
The Northern Auras cast their light ...

From a darkened sky of deep blue,
The air turned to a purple hue,
Then threw a whisk of lime green,
That whisped across the heights,
That hissed into their sight.

An entry so brilliantly bright.

Each raised their head from low,
A half-neck to peer,
All eyes to rise.

Through atmosphere, he appeared
As a grand illusion.
First a giant sharp shard,
Jagged across his path,
To a scintillation of crystals
That circled his very all,
To Earth then they'd fall.

You could almost hear them sprinkle.

Wings that floated as they rose,
Caught the electric light.
Even though gleaming white,
Colours glimpsed the feathers' lines.

The half-lit side of a stallion's
Angular chest, that continued
To his fine muscular neck.

A mane that skewed in superb flight,
As though waving strands upright.

Nostrils that flared to freshen air,
And as they blew,
A whinny and a wheeze,
Smiled a welcoming tease.

Enlightened, the sheer fantasy,
Hooves that danced a rhapsody.

All attentioned-heads up high,
Some reared at the dreamt-excite.

He's finally here, without invite.

The disciple to The Messiah,
The opened heavens were on fire.

....

For he was a beautiful image,
To which planets stop and stare,
And with a flick of forelock hair,
A charisma that couldn't compare.

He told of the special foal up high,
He, winged stallion, flew to Earth,
Delivering great news, as his serf,
He told of the heavens' mirth.

All whinny to the galloping cryer
Of great news to The Unicorn's birth.

2.
He told of a sugar cube life,
Beyond the fields, bare and dry.

"Don't let humans be your master,
  Canter great meadows of golden pasture."

3.
The lone donkey didn't quite know,
Not to get too involved,
Kept his nose to low.

Now an elder, rings to eyes,
Nothing in life was a surprise.

For carrots were charity,
After a stroke to his nose,
They all laughed at his beard,
Sad mouth, that ugliness showed.

4.
To the next field over the weeds,
Were the prettiest Arabs that feed.

Coiffured, plaited manes.
Beautiful pulled tails.
A slim head to fine jaw,
A make-up life seemed the law.

Donkey had looked over before.

They worshipped the angel;
The gleaming winged-stallion,
And seeming to love his shimmy,
Believed The Unicorn explained.

For the chosen one with horn to head,
Would welcome them all to
Heavenly-golden pastures,
When field life turned to their death.

They fell for his charming whinny.
The light of eyes, misted breath.

They ate at the grass field church,
They looked up to the aura they saw,
An enlightenment to the above,
So, would no longer be slaved.

The higher life that they craved.

For they were all groomed,
Their beauty presumed.
Best for toed-dressage,
But knew a greater place loomed.

Their saddles handmade,
With manes and tails of braid.

Whinny to the winged angel's shimmy.

The Rainbow Unicorn is The Messiah,
He, the hope, the wantened desire.

5.
His nose snuffled the daisies,
That were petal-wet to the last rain.
The summer field, grass-bare,
Nettled-leaves to the fence wire.

This was a bad day;
Head to low,
Pin eyes, no glow,

And the passing walkers
Thought him lazy.
His mane spiked,
Big rounded nose.

When his head was half-raised,
He could see over the greener hedge,
A little way past gathering weeds.

And he dreamed of the sugar cube life,
Lived by the timid-legged mares;
Sunday best, plaited hair.
Their tails constant pulled,
Angel-groomed, with such care.

So,
He started to think something was missing,
Even though happy, eating all day,
He thought of the colours in the sky,
When the winged-angel broke the night.

The harshness of the bedding straw,
Yet he was promised hectares of hay.

"Never trot on another's acres,
  Was the word of The Unicorn maker."

His mind high-kneed the vision fields,
With thousands of like-donkeys;

He handsome, the same as they,
Each with Ned heads, proud,
Large curved ears forward,
Smiling with a glint to teeth.
Happy eyes, wide,
To all buck together,
And say "He was right."

The winged-male angel
Of energied light -
Their bare fields, grass-endowed.

"Pull not your master's chariot,
  For he bears stick before any carrot."

Their destiny was now defined,
Their mental health so stabled.

According to The Nose Bag of Life.

Nobody would ever see the proof,
But they danced to tapping of the angel's hoof.

6.
Oh disbeliever !

As seasons passed through colder nights,
Donkey and the church of mares,
And every dosing field equine,
Now and then,
Could look up and see the electric sky.

Statued-silhouette poses,
Stretched-necks long,
Their up-pointed heads,
Looking above the boundary fence.

Noses blowing whisp snow air.

Colours reflect in dark chestnut eyes.

What more did they need
To know, than The Rainbow Unicorn
Was looking over their grazing-lives.

....

Donkey, as his first act of faith,
Took to one knee, ... head high,
And to The Unicorn's festive display,

With heart of the brave,

Began to bray.

Your family history is important.
It gives you a sense of being.
Each person will remember
Points in time; good and bad,
Where their mind's clock stops.

The Gaberdine

The War Years

1.

The babe held to the elbow crux,
Morning after the hoar frost.
The weather now to an air sleet.
He bound in bedding cloth,
His nose of redden' cold.
Father's coat round to his head,
Droplets settle, again they froze.

But he lied in safety's love,
The week after war's last day,
Scene, stationary, black and white.
Father, flat cap donned,
Shading eyes of grey.
If not so cold would cry a tear,
His pain hard-stilled head to toe.

But what that gabardine coat did know;
Trenches, the officer bold,
Regiment badge pinned to hat,
The tweed, threaded, longed.
It bore smells of war;
Ammunition-coked.
In pocket, his wife's photo,
To rear, written, the heart-torn note.

The raised lump to his throat.

The babe grew to fatherless-child,
Four lapels kept flat,
Hung below his regiment cap.
The sentiment bemothed.
Mind memories untold,
Still to smell his father's dread,
The heritage to which he dotes.

To pocket, love and kisses,
To mind, the greatest troth.
His mother's sepia image,
Tiny, worn and cracked.

Her eyes were bright,
Her smile, purest white,
Skin that held no woes.

....

From wearing his innocence hood,
In the trench coat, he now stood.

The eleventh hour.
The eleventh day.
The eleventh month.

That badged-cap under arm.
That medal, colour to breast.

His walk, as his father walked.
He thought, how his father talked.

But the instilled image to mind;
The tear to his cold pater's eyes.

Lying in the crux of the coat,
Ears warmed by twirled thread.

His mother had already died.

2.
Each year he wore the gaberdine with respect
As each late regiment laid their poppy ring.

The slow walk to the memorial's steps.

And before the mute crowd of hundreds,
A kneel, as the commemoration was leant.

To then stand back, to remove father's cap,
That was pressed to the crux of his elbow,

His hands to low with fingers crossed.
One moment's recollection for his loss.

To heart, mother's war-torn note kept,
To pocket the chained, initialled-watch,

That he took out, his right arm passed across,
The hands at the time when war years slept.

3.
The belted-coat lay across his bed,
With little fray to the threading edge.

His hand flat smooth to the lapels,
Rose to feel the collar's curve nape.

And centrally sewn into the steep,
With his initials, Burberry's label.

The penned ink from nineteen fourteen,
Hallmark of his priceless gaberdine.

And gathered as part of sentiment,
The smell of the wartime's scent.

4.
The lad married young as a late teen,
The first of his family not far behind.

And his son had clear blue eyes,
The same as mother's photo to mind.

He, a conscript to the second war,
His elder's coat went on the tour.

And he saw what his father saw,
And fought like his father fought.

And felt what his pater had felt,
His security still, was the buckle belt.

5.
Many years later he returned home,
The gaberdine as a hero's cloak.

Wearing his father's long sleeves,
Hugged his family in great relief.

And his son cried as he had cried,
He lifted him to sit to his hip.

The gaberdine held him secure fast,
Just as his early memory did last.

And in May's morning chill of cold,
What happened on tour ... remained untold.

6.
He felt the length of coat on his bed,
The smooth of the back to its tail.

The post trauma came to his head.

And he tried like his father tried,
To remove the spoils from his mind.

From innocence to great manhood,
The test of war bayed as he stood.

But the coat meant he wasn't afraid,
As his mind's comfort for another day.

The cloak still ammunition-coked,
A tear to blubber as he choked.

As a hand to his father was love,
His, slipped inside history's gloves.

With the watch wound to continue time,
In hope the memories would pass away.

7.
The enemy, a squadron of drones,
To grey skies, the allies honed.
To bare fields, every soldier prone,
Life's flesh torn from their bodies' bones.

Then in the twilight of the dawn,
As the sun rose to the morn ...

An eerie silence.

The clear blue skies.

But his ears heard the night before.

The allied troops, bloody torn.

8.
In the quiet of November's grief,
Stood more of his father's belief.

He now walked as his pater walked,
And wore his own medal to chest.

Own badged-cap to his breast.

Laid the wreath to memorial's steps,
Still holding post trauma, he wept;

The drones of planes, to mind crept.

He had sworn the oath his father swore,
Not knowing what his elder had borne.

There were no glories to unfold.
Just the images ... that stayed untold.

....

The watch wound daily to continue time,
His mother's eyes framed on the side.

What that gaberdine did know,
Hung to the wardrobe, as stowed,

In hope the war years would pass away.

....

His coping had nil effect.

The squadrons sewn to grey skies.

Early morning, balling-smoke, plumed.

Even though his mother smiled,

There could be no bluer day.

The Maypole

With tiny gold bells to their wrists,
The high-pitched chinkles as they skipped.

Wartime was over, mid-November past,
The celebration of May, marked the day.

To the village green, home-made tables,
Cotton cloths were then over-laid.
And triangle bunting frisked the air,
That looped from lamppost to post.
The up-masted rippling union flag,
Military brass to the bandstand played.

To the centre field, the main displays.

And the sun shone throughout the day,
The proud music, resoundingly gay.

Each child with paper garlands to necks,
Each with shorts and ankle-socked legs.

The maypole reached up to high,
One would squint at the bluest sky.

The yearly-festival of mid-spring,
Now also marked another thing ...

He remembered,

To the vast green grasses,
Each child chinkled,
The smiles so wide,
As they started to sing.

Dancing with streamers to their hands,
They skipped to the jollied hop jazz band.

To skip and bound and dance and sing;
Skip to coloured-flowers of spring.

The war children round the ring, prance,
To their freedom, they smiled and danced.

Round and round such joy they'd bring,
To each soldier that landed beach sand.

As though motion waves to the seas,
Coloured streamers, undulating, fanned.

....

Then he looked up to see Daddy's eyes,
That wept a small tear of self-pride.

He uniformed, again, brushed pristine.
In warmth, the arm-folded gaberdine.

For years with his young life chanced,
Four years, the trenches were manned.

....

As the music quietly closed,

Each child to the maypole lowed.

The young hopes ... to a walk slowed.

Their longed-ribbons spiralled true;
Patterned the colours, red, white and blue.

....

That year the country turned the tide,
The allied forces had saved their lives.

The memory to his eye twinkled.

The glow of light through paper strands.

Undulating, twisted, as they flew.

The trombone and French horn blew.

The happiness of hearing the chinkles.

The children singing to late spring.

Written large to one overhanging cloth,
In red and blue, written, 1919.

....

Ice cream dripping to his little hand.

Optimistic was the cloudless sky.

But as a child, he couldn't understand.

The day's image made his eyes smile,
The spirals to be his colourful dreams.

The Nightmare

As darkness fell, his covered-eyes,
The years after he fought for lives.

The hanging bulb engrained to his lids,
As the light turned off its switch.

To his pillow, beautiful blue skies,
The background to the maypole's ties.

And he saw paper tapers, long,
Pulled by children in full song.

Undulating in sunlight.

Skipping to the grassy field,
Chuckling, at the spiral peeled.

Giggling, as the threads were stitched.

"One, two, skip under you,
  Three, four, over your head.

  One, two, sunlight through white,
  As a wave, the colours bright.

  One, two, threading the blue,
  Three, four, beau ribbons red."

Laughing with whiter smiles,
Laughing with eyes of light.

One, two ...
Three, four ...

The brass band played jazz galore.

But
His mind trashed the dreams of streams,
Unravelling the spiral at its seams.

The skies turned to war grey.
The single note of enemies' planes,
Engulfing-smoke spiralled to high,
After burning throughout the night.
The eeriness of the morning after,
Deafened-ears still heard them fight.

And he fought like his father fought,
Was distraught as his father fraught.

And in his black and white fright,
The gaberdine coat forever worn.

His mind and heart of scorn ...

Then a gestured smile of slight,
He remembered his mother's eyes.

She, the young beautiful bride,
A face that showed no woes.

Her smile, the brightest white,
Though the photo small and torn.

And his mind as his elder's mind,
Traumatised by the wartime sights.

His sanity fled as his father's had fled,
His heart bled as his father was dead.

The beautiful tapers to the sky,
The chinkles of May Day pride ...

Seemed to his dream denied.

They laughed with innocent smiles.

The colours twisted as they wove.

The band played the last long note ...
That continued to war planes' drones.

And, as the skipping children did sing,

He looked high …

To a tall lean man stood upright,

His dark quiffed hair, hand-greased,

The last puff of his smoke released.

Cigarette hanging to the mouth's crease.

With a tear balled to gloried-eyes,

Hardly a movement of thinned-lips,

He looked to his child, admired.

…

The silver fob now stopped on right time.

…

To then whisper, … through half a mouth,

"My darling boy, … God save The King."

Who are the good people ?
The self-titled
'Reverends of religion' ?
Those with more money ?
Media stars and actors ?
The monarchy of a country ?

The Palace View

The Sentry Gates

I asked him.
He replied,

"I'm waiting to see The Queen."

One morning while commuting the city.

On good days, sat to the wall,
On less ones, bottom to floor.

As years went on, I realised
That,

As I walked streets, train to train,
Each weekday I was doing the same,

That went to each month, each year -
The street man was still there.

I asked him.
He replied,

"At 11, they are changing the guard."

Each morning travelling to the city,
On good days, his words touched,
On bad days, he'd drank too much.

As years went on, I realised
That,

The more that I talked, less the strain,
A surprise, his drink wasn't to blame.

He fought in the war,
A loyalist ... or royalist,
Dependent on the day.

"I'm waiting to meet The Queen."

He told me that she waved on the balcony;
Waved to everyone, especially he.

And before he said, I crouched,
And asked,

"Why do you sit before the palace of wonder,
  When there is food and bedding yonder?"

He looked, red underlined,
With crackle-glazed eyes,
Filled with brew overnight,
A slur to lips, but quite polite.

With lisp to a whisper,
"I am one hundredth to the throne,
  My tree of relatives, publicly known.

  I sit and wait to the sentry gates,
  Soldiers in jackets lovely and warm,
  The high bearskins to heads worn.

  And when I am the country's king on throne,
  I'll be paying their wages, also boy pages,
  With servants, I'll have the grandest home."

I asked where was his home?

He told, he served The Falklands War,
He stirred about year 1982.

When he came back he lost his wife,
Lost love, and started living alone.

He then looked up, fright to eye,
As a low helicopter passed us by.

"I saw a sea of beautiful flowers
  To the gate when Lady Diana died.'

I counted how many years were cost.

"For now, here is my home.
  I have the best of views,
  I smile, as the royals drive through."

....

And, as I stood,
I saw an old man,
Grey matted-beard,
Unkempt for most his years,

An old blue Parker coat with hood.

....

" Where do you live ?" he asked.

" I bet you have a big house,
  A beautiful wife as a spouse.
  A girl, a boy, that you spoil,
  To your own castle, a king ?"

He had asked,
I almost said,

Then thought my answer as obscene.

I gestured money to his open cap.

He smiled, few teeth, gaps between.

"I will send you an invite when I'm there." ...

Admiring-eyes circled, many times,
That glazed through to a stare.

"I'll wave from the balcony to crowds,
  The whole place loud, coloured-flags,"

"Did I tell you ?
  I'm hundredth in line, after The Queen."

The Flags

The crowd flags are waving,
Each one, minute, to The Queen's palace union.
They emulate their higher view.

The Queen's flag is waving unto thou.
One knows she is residing in town.

The proud crowds are cheering,
But royalty is not cheering with you.

They stand with a smile,
Their pretences adhered.
They look down on
The minion population;
The miners,
The labourers,
The sweepers,
And corner shopkeepers.

Royalty waving straight hands,
Angled to the strict rules,
Ones' faces, each endeared,
Using courtesy as tools.

The drivers,
The caterers,
The bakers,
That make up their great nation.
Fishers,
Finishers,
Farmers,
That stand beyond gatekeepers.

Hopers waving, hands fanned,
Faster, as though fuelled.
Their excitement so clear,
Such expression so true.

Ten thousand flags fluttering,
Yet one might think it oh so crude.

Another View

The balcony, used by the elite few,
And I imagined the view ...

The crowds, from far, that travelled,
All needed to look up as a hope,
To see what they would never be.

Images of a gilded show.

Kings and queens look down
With ermine-lined gowns.
Their own coat of arms,
A belief of their charms.

But, is the wave a greeting ?
Or from higher to lower,
A confidence repleted ?

If there was no palace, no gates,
There would be no reasons
To line the paved-streets;
A proud of people to wait.

....

And some stand to The Pope,
He in the path of their view,
While they look to Heaven, higher.

The papal tiara that he wears,
Makes him a prior being,
As ''God's words'', he shares.

....

Each mind is made to think higher;
Whether the balustraded-balcony,
Or to those with more money.

The magpies allude to silver jewels.

....

The mountain summit a perfect a view,
The peak only stood by one or two.

And the rainbow is just a vision,
That stands to weather's indecision.

The diamond dream in the sky,
Grows smaller as they fly to high.

....

Would it be easier to say that
Everything is below us ?

Would it help to what bestows us ?

The clergy and those of the crown,
Are very happy looking down.

Amused as one curtsies or bows,
With kisses to The Father's hand.

....

The donkey doesn't have a unicorn sky,
Or see the stallion's wings to the wind ...

To be just who he is,
Working sack to back,
But then ... looks down at the ass.

....

The purveyed paranoia,
Is set to destroy us,

But we use self-delusion every day.

....

For the whole world
Is every religion's city,
Many a language spoken.

And every no-man's
Is every man's land,
The largest communities broken.

For every mother and father tree
Are part of our bigger being.

Do you not think they cry,
After centuries, they're cut for our need ?

Their forest world city slaughtered ...
For humanity's handsome greed.

And hope has to run through
The whole of one's life;
The new year to be better than the last,
Or future generations to
Make the world a better place.
Then,
There is lottery's chance.

The Storeys of Tenement Lives

Admiring the monied-city
To the far horizon,
She stood with the balconied-view.

A concrete block of thirty storeys,
Each one council-given,
Each person a liven-story.

Below, from the money prism,
They looked up at her life, pitied ...

Their lives compared,
Huge bonuses, shared

... Not even knowing the wife, riven.

Her bank balance, pennies few,
She dreamed the lottery life.

One ticket

Was it so much to ask ?
A complete world contrast.

One ticket to the golden path.

To get to the view, she saw,
She had walked up inclining steps,
One by one,
Shopping to each clenched-hand,
Floor to floor,
As though conquering Everest ...

To the view that her life was less.

....

So came the dreamt day.
The note of golden pay.

The ticket.

With six numbers crossed,
The bonus was ringed ...

The ticket, for what she prayed.

....

She laughed, she smiled,
She pranced, she danced,

She dreamed, she whiled,
The end to poverty, played.

The millions were God-given.

....

Each year she had looked to the city,
Resenting their salaries, glittered,

So,
She stood to her balcony, high,
To say a quick last goodbye
And fluttered the ticket in hand;
A smiled gloat to her whole
Life lived, ... sorely embittered.

One ticket.

She dreamed of her mansion, grand.

With her fingers crossed,
Sang, "five golden rings".

One ticket,

That, as it fluttered,

One second,

Her new life stuttered,

As she gaily singed.
The winner caught the wind ...

As a leaf to the breeze,
Slowly,
It floated to the right,
Slowly,
It floated to the left ...

Her face was frozen, aghast.
Her life stories flew past.

The ticket.

It twirled, it swirled,

She ran, and ran, step to step,
Thirty storeys of concrete glory,

The ticket, to be lost, bayed.

She ran, and ran, floor to floor,
Like she had never, ever, ran before.

....

As a leaf to the breeze,
Lowing,
It floated to the right,
Flowing,
It floated to the left ...

To the ground it curled.

....

She ran and ran, past each door,
Some had her lucky numbers adorned:

44 was the bonus ball.

31 was her date of birth.

30, the year she married.

20, just crossed as luck.

12, the coldest month born.

10, the prime minister's door.

Just as a numbered path
Descending to Hell's grief,

Number 1 was a kick in the teeth.

....

Her ticket fell on flowing gutter rain,
To curl around and lick the bars,
The water glugging as it laughed,
To fall down the roadside's drain.

She cried as though insane.
Then looked up at her concrete life,
Not to think that others were more poor.

....

Life's path can give lottery's chance,
But never forget the staircase of pain.

....

A concrete block of thirty storeys,
Each one council-given,
Each person a liven-story.

Her life of pennies, few.
Wind-littered was the chance that flew.

Each person ... a living story.
Back down to earth after a moment's glory.

The Final Thought

The Palace Viewed

One morning while commuting the city,
As I walked from station to station,

In the crawling hub of corporations,

Out the side of my eyes' view,
The street man wasn't there.

The wall was not sat to.
The pavement, no belongings.

I thought,
Not assumed.

I looked up and across the street,
Looked down to my stationary feet.

The street man ... wasn't there !

My thoughts stared to a glare.

I looked around to the palace,
Over the high walls, gated.

Did he really get to where he, himself, related ?

I overheard one person to another.
They said the street man was dead.

....

So, I sat on his patch.
Sat, back to the wall.
Sat to the cold stone ...

With ladies made-up for the office,
Gents dressed, the city to impress.
Hundreds passing my high-bent legs.

At such a low height, so alone.

I, in mind, had levelled the seesaw of respect.

And I looked through the sentry gates,
To then wipe a tear to his one dream ...

He, to wave on the balcony, above ...

Just wanting to be loved.

He shouldn't have needed a crowd,
To make him feel as proud.

His ever-thought of elation,
Yet, knew not one of his relations.

If only I had talked to him more,
And held his wanten hand,

··· Instead of looking down.

I hadn't ever asked of his name.
My cocktail of shame and self-blame.

But now I saw his view,

It shared by many more ... than one or two.

Mother Tree 5

"Good morning Mother Tree on such a nice day."
He really did feel good, as he walked down the dell.
When he finally saw Mater, ...
His mind enlightened, ... his whole heart to her spell.

Under bright green of spring's leaves,
Where daffodils trump in glade light,

He walked with his son to his hand;
His young and heir to dwell.

Years had passed since his kiss, last.

He stood to Mother Tree,
His hand firm to her girth,
And introduced his boy
To his constant, ... that still believed.

As his lad's neck reached high.
As his jaw dropped to wide ...

"This my son, is Mother Tree.

  It is she,

  Who was here decades before we were made,
  And will be here when we, both to rest, laid.

  For I cried and cried
  That she might die
  Because of mankind."

A disbelief to his young mind,
A wonderment to his eyes.

The man arced his arms
Around her mighty trunk,
Holding his son's hand
To the other side ...

"This is how we behold history."

"This is how we protect the future."

"And when I am long gone,
  You should stand to the wrongs.

  For in her lifetime,

  You are one of her million nuts,
  Off many thousand twigs,
  From her hundreds of branches,
  That come off one-hearted trunk.

  In the whole of history, we are minions.

  History is not your text book or Bible.
  They are humanity's tiny stories,
  That try to prove our self-glories ...

  Yet most show ... we played a bad part."

....

And countries were still fighting.

The holy caliphate with reprisals.

Capitalists surfed the wave of money.

They all expected a better tomorrow.

....

As they walked away, for another day,
Holding hands, the boy looked back ...

The leaves changed in the sunlight,
As though she gave respectful requite.

He saw a tree that was a giant to he;
One with a character and a life.

....

Behind was an ever-stability;
Optimism in fine, gladed-light,
So he could walk forward
With a more positive stride;

An optimism to run through the family tribe.

Nature's open-hinged, wood-carved trove.

It had no need of money's ability.
A forest of gleaming crowned-jewels;

Thousands of leaves of jade,
Spring flowers, cut diamond-made,
Burnt-amber, a ground sheeted-bed laid.

Fanned shaft-light as champagne poured,
To his wonder-filled eyes, adored.

....

And though he didn't quite understand,
He still wished her a fond goodbye.

Her baby nut in a million.

Written during 2020 when the world fought against COVID-19.

The year when countries talked to each other
In a war played without guns and ammunition.
Each man, woman and child became vulnerable.
Standing apart was standing together.
You could own great jewels and wealth, but die to the virus.
Yet, leaders still thought it couldn't infect them. It did.
Each colour or race were not exempt.
No prayer, in any church, could save the day.

We realised that to be with, to touch and hug
Your loved ones was of the greatest importance;
To see the children grow day by day,
To see your grandparents before they passed away.

Yet, we soon will be back to our selfish ways.

This is history.

In the whole of the world's history ... we are minions.

A little Extra.

The Forest of Love

They dug into the earth,
Fifty family and friends,
Their blades of spades.
Each one knew the same man.

With love, each made a hole,
And planted new roots.
Fifty family and friends,
Each one had the same plan.

Each sapling, young of seed,
Each one a memory tree,
That would grow and grow.

Each spring, blossom of white,
Each summer, leaf of green,
Each autumn, leaves below.

Each year branch to branch,
Each tree grew to an arch,
To touch the next one's span.

They held hands to remember this man.
The next fifty to his lady neighbour,
Then fifty to the dead child to her.

The COVID forest of love
Spread across the home land.
Spread over our whole world.
From man of white,
To man of black,
Woman of brown,
Red-skinned child.

A world rebuilt so we could breathe.

Never forget our losses,
Each of them the virus need.

Stand, not to shed such blame,
Your death, could be the same.

In each leaf, a memory believed.

....

Every felled Amazon tree,
A skeleton to its death.
Each dies to plague of man.

Each one ... a cut of its breath.

Each next tree, stands ... to the axemen, bereaved.

The Amazon plague goes year on year,
Not just for our natural need ...

Millions of trees lost to man's greed.